MW01630061

OLD FLORIDA POTTERY

Orlando Potteries vase. Circa 1922.

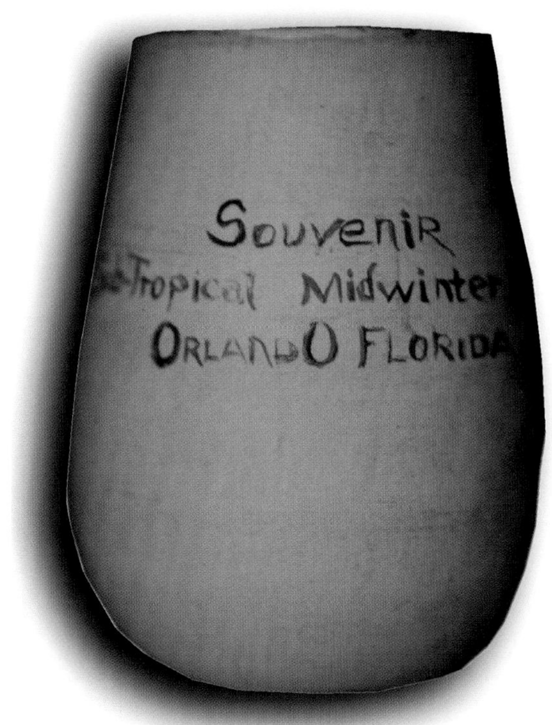

Souvenir
Tropical Midwinter
ORLANDO FLORIDA

POTTERS IN PARADISE

A Collector's Guide to Makers, Marks and History of

OLD FLORIDA

POTTERY

1859-1966

ALFRED R. FRANKEL, M.D.

Blue Dome Press
St. Pete Beach, Florida

ISBN# 0-9672662-0-3

Library of Congress Catalog Card Number: 99-64637

Additional copies may be purchased through:
    Blue Dome Press
    Post Office Box 46675
    St. Pete Beach, Florida 33741-6675
    727-367-5380

Pottery shown on jacket is from Manatee River Pottery, Graack Pottery, Orlando Potteries
and Kohler Pottery in St. Petersburg.

Design by: Douglas M. Eason, Havana, Florida

CONTENTS

Chapters

ACKNOWLEDGEMENTS

This book would not have been written without the friendship of Clark and Vicky McLean, Tampa pottery dealers who first introduced me to Manatee River and Graack pottery in 1985. My interest aroused, I began to search for more information on the potteries and found it in microfilm of the *"Manatee River Journals"* at the Bradenton Public Library. One discovery followed the other from Bradenton to Tampa to St. Petersburg, Orlando, Ocala, Lake Butler, Pensacola, Bluff Springs and Palm Beach. My knowledge grew thanks to the small flame lit by Clark and Vicky. Clark passed away in 1997. He is missed.

My thanks to Don Fredgant, a gentleman I've never met, who published the first articles on the Knox Hill, Pensacola, Lake Butler and Crary Potteries in *The Antiques Journal* in 1980-1981. Fredgants writings were the first serious attempt to define pottery making here in Florida.

Sincere thanks go to the descendants of Florida potters who agreed to meet with me and share their memories, including Madelyn Graack Peterson, Alvin Kohler, Ruth Hickman, Mrs. Dean Crary and Mrs. Hal York Maines. My sincere thanks go to Wilbur Casper, the last of the early Florida potters, for his reminiscences of Merritt Island Pottery.

Thanks to the historical society curators who shared their time, knowledge and pottery, particularly Peggy Somerville and Marlene Frick of the Manatee County Historical Society, Betty Johnson of the Pensacola Historical Society, Kerry Kennedy and Frank Menendez of the Orange County Historical Society, Neil Collier of the Alger-Sullivan Historical Society, Kristen Gaspari of the Palm Beach Historical Society, Peggy McCall of the Boca Raton Historical Society, Chris LaRoche of the Okaloosa-Walton History Museum and Mr. Bruce Graetz, Curator, Museum of Florida History, Tallahassee, Florida.

Thanks are due to William B. Rae, Bruce Mozert and Al Scudder, all of Ocala who shared their memories of Henry Graack, to Harold Gillis for his help in finding Knox Hill and to Charles Adler of Davis Island, Tampa for his memories of his friend, Royal Hickman.

My friendship with Florida antique dealers Michael Turbeville of Tampa and Larry Roberts of Micanopy has long been a source of support and shared knowledge for what at times seemed our quixotic love of Florida art and antiques. I thank them for their friendship. Thanks to Keith Kuperman and Eileen Snyder leading dealers in Haeger and Royal Hickman Pottery who were helpful in obtaining rare pieces of Florida Hickman pottery and for their knowledge of Hickman glazes and clay.

Diane Marcou, of St.Petersburg, edited this manuscript and made many suggestions that make it more readable. Her help is greatly appreciated.

Finally my love and thanks to my wife, Barbara Shehane Frankel, for her love and understanding when I was off antiquing or in a library, and to my son, Brian Frankel, who may someday write his own books about Florida.

INTRODUCTION

Why a book about early Florida pottery? When I moved back to Florida in 1980 the words Florida and antiques didn't seem to fit. The state was too new and remnants of early Florida culture rare. I thought that anything old or of historical interest found here was from another state. Time and study have taught me that this is not true. Florida has a broad material cultural heritage that is not well known today. This is particularly true of early Florida pottery. County historical societies have limited knowledge of pottery produced locally and antique dealers who specialize in pottery know vaguely about Graack and Silver Springs pottery.

Archaeologists have defined cultural periods as essentially ceramic periods. W.H. Holmes, writing in *Earthenware of Florida, Collections of Clarence B. Moore* (a study of native Florida Indian pottery) states, "It is on ceramic evidence perhaps more than any other that we depend for solutions of problems of time, people and culture."

Florida pottery reflects the lives of the pioneers who founded this state. Nancy Sweezy, author of *RAISED IN CLAY, THE SOUTHERN POTTERY TRADITION*, University of North Carolina Press, describes pottery use in the South. "Food and liquid had to be contained and preserved, water cooled and transported, oil burned for light. Basins were needed for washing; containers for soap; stewpots and bread pans for open hearth cooking; and pitchers, mugs, and bowls for the table. Milk was a farm staple, and crocks were needed for cream rising and butter storage and churns for butter making. Meat was salted, vegetables pickled, lard and tallow stored in large jars; cane syrup, vinegar, wine, and liquor were put in jugs; fruit and jams preserved in small jars. The potters also made sieves, water coolers, funnels, measuring cups, baby bottles, animal feeders, chimney flues, spittoons, chamber pots, inkwells, clay pipes, playing marbles called 'peedabs' and grave markers." Clearly, to understand our world and our place in it Floridians must study our pottery, our art, our material cultural heritage.

Florida is now the third largest state in the United States but, incredibly, anyone who tries to find a history of our early material culture will find almost nothing. *Florida Visionaries: 1870-1930*, published by the University Presses of Florida in 1989, helped to define some of our earliest artists. *Images of Old Florida* (1890-1950) published by the Boca Raton Museum of Art, expanded our knowledge of Florida artists. *Celebrating Florida, Works of Art from the Vickers Collection*, introduces other Florida artists. *Florida Quilts* by Charlotte Williams teaches us about early Florida quilt makers and Dorothy Downs, author of *Art of Florida Seminole and Miccosukee Indians*, explores native Seminole artistic traditions. Beyond these few pioneering books and pamphlets there is little to tell Floridians about their material cultural heritage.

The lack of cultural definition here in Florida today is not unlike that in the South back in 1949, when, at an Antiques Forum held in Colonial Williamsburg, speakers reported that they could find no group of Southern furniture comparable in quality or quantity to that produced in any one of the Northern states. A speaker remarked that, "little of artistic merit was made south of Baltimore." This disturbing lack of knowledge led to a major exhibition, at the Virginia Museum of Fine Arts in January 1952, of Southern furniture produced from 1640 to 1820 and later the founding of The Museum of Early Southern Decorative Arts in Winston Salem, North Carolina.

Many books have now been written on Southern material culture, but there is little in them about Florida. This is partly the result of Florida being essentially a wilderness until the building of the Flagler East Coast Railroad and the Plant System of railroads and steamships between 1885 and 1912. Jessie Poesch's book *The Art of the Old South 1560-1860* (1983 Harrison House) contains only three references to Florida. *Southern Folk Art* by Cynthia Elyce Rubin (1985 Oxmoor House) while including Florida on a map of the South contains no examples of Florida folk art. Robert Morton's *Southern Antique Folk Art* also has nothing on Florida.

The general vacuum relating to Florida cultural heritage and its pottery has led me to write this book. I am no art scholar. My qualifications to compile this history include my love of this state, a desire to see its culture celebrated and my interest in the potters as evidenced by first hand interviews with their descendants and ten years of library research. A study of utilitarian and decorative pottery produced in Florida since statehood is just a small part of our rich cultural heritage which needs to be explored.

Florida pottery is American folk art at its best. Made of Florida clay and the sweat of pioneers, it reflects in its shiny alkaline and Albany slip glazes the lives and dreams of its creators. The story begins in 1859 at Knox Hill near DeFuniak Springs in the Florida panhandle. Florida had been a state for just fourteen years and its pioneers were struggling to survive when the bugle call of the Civil War was heard. The war tore the Union in half and was probably responsible for the closing of the Knox Hill pottery. The war sent one future Pensacola potter south from his home in Michigan to Nashville, Tennessee while a youthful future potter living near Gainesville enlisted with the 7th Florida Infantry.

The first Florida potteries produced the jugs, churns and food storage jars needed to survive in the wilderness. When the Civil War ended and railroads began to push south into the state bringing more immigrant settlers and then winter tourists, the needs of the people changed and Addison Mizner, an architect from California, began to produce roof and floor tiles and decorative pottery for the homes he was building in Palm Beach and Mary Ward, a Tennessean, arrived in Bradentown with thoughts of producing decorative pottery for the home.

I have written about the potters that I believe are important to this state's pottery history. These potters were not the only potters in Florida. In Pensacola there is a road called, "Old Pottery Road." This road is far from the downtown site of Kohler's Southern Pottery Works and indicates that there was a pottery here, possibly in the 1930s and perhaps run by the Pace family. Floramics was a Tampa pottery run by Elise Frank, a Tampa artist, and her brother, in the 1950s. They produced attractive pottery and their work needs to be documented. Mark Dixon Dodd, a prominent St. Petersburg artist, had a pottery on Fourth St. North in the early 1950s and Seminole Indians briefly produced pottery for sale to tourists. These potteries all need to be documented. Work still needs to be done.

The study of Florida pottery has been a joyful experience for me. I hope the reader will share in this joy. Eve Alsman Fuller, who was active in the art community in St. Petersburg in the 1910-1930 period, wrote in her art column for the *St. Petersburg Times*, "A community, be it large or small, should receive the creative efforts of its citizens in a prideful manner, tendering due honor and helpfulness; participating joyously in the results of the efforts." Let us begin joyously the celebration of Florida pottery.

A Mizner cast
stone Lamp.
Total height 30
inches, height
of case stone
15 1/4 inches,
width 9 inches.
Los Manos
Pottery. ca
1918-1933.
Courtesy,
Boca Raton
Historical
Society.

To my parents, Ceil and Bernard Frankel,
who gave me life, love and Florida.

"All this of pot and Potter-Tell me then
Who is the Potter, pray, and who the Pot?"
—The Rubaiyat of Omar Khayyam

Chapter One

A wheel thrown pitcher with a clear glaze over a reddish grey brown ovoid body with applied handle and pouring spout. Four incised horizontal bands about the neck. Embossed TB ODOM with periods placed at the upper, rather than the lower, part of the mark. Height 8 3/4 inches, base 5 3/4 inches, mouth 4 1/2 inches. One-quarter inch indentation at base. Turnley and Odom Pottery, Knox Hill, Florida. Circa 1859. Courtesy, Okaloosa-Walton Historical Museum, Valparaiso, Florida.

Turnley and Odom Pottery, Knox Hill 1859

The war cries of the Creek and Seminole Indians had finally quieted in West Florida. The Yuchee Indians had moved south to the Everglades and in a hand to hand, life or death struggle Indian Joe, a raiding Indian had been killed and his sons run off. A temporary peace had come to the land between the Yellow and Choctawhatchie Rivers in the Florida Panhandle.

The first Scotch settlers named that territory "Walton" in honor of General Jackson's aide Colonel George Walton and, "from 1840 to 1860, there was no county of Walton's area whose people were more happy and contented, more healthy and strong, more advanced in true religion and culture, and no more prosperous in material wealth, than the people of this little bit of territory." (1)

In the fall of 1848 the Reverend John Newton arrived in Pensacola and was convinced by the Scottish elders of Walton County living at Uchee Anna near present day DeFuniak Springs, to start a school at Knox Hill. Newton, a Pennsylvanian and a graduate of Amherst College, began teaching school in a simple log cabin, "the Henry School House that stood near a spring northeast of the Morrison place at Old Knox Hill." (2) This spring, known as Turnlee Spring, would later provide convenient water for a pottery.

In 1858 Newton married Margaret Campbell and the school was moved several hundred yards south and west down Knox Hill. (3) (4) In ten years the Knox Hill Academy grew to become the educational center of West Florida.

The steady rapid growth and the results in education became the wonder of West Florida and South Alabama. Many

An olive green spotted alkaline glazed stoneware storage jar, signed in glaze M. M. Odom on the side. Height 14 1/2 inches, diameter 9 inches. Knox Hill Pottery, Walton County, Florida. Circa. 1859-1860. Accession from F. E. Buchanan. Courtesy: Museum of Florida History. Catalogue number 50309.

would come to see the Knox Hill Academy and the wonderful teacher. The other schools mentioned that dotted the Valley melted away under its shining light. Those that lived too far away to send their children from home and were able to board, sent them, and those not able, moved nearby. But a great many of the pupils, especially the larger ones, were transient borders, from Pensacola, Vernon, Marianna, Quincy, and Geneva, Alabama, and some from Georgia and from the wealthy farmers around these towns. (5)

Along with the flourishing Academy, Knox Hill had a lawyer, W.C. McLean, and a doctor, A. Gillis. J.H. Colton's Map of Florida for the year 1856 reveals that Uchee Anna and Knox Hill were two of only three towns in Walton County. There is no question that in the years 1850 to 1860 Knox Hill was an important center of Walton County life and it was here in 1859 that the first pottery in Florida was started.

The importance of a pottery to early Florida settlers is clear. People living on the Florida frontier in 1859 required little in the way of money. Folks grew and stored their own food and on rare trips to Pensacola purchased the coffee, salt and flour they could not grow. Cattle raising provided fresh meat, butter, sweet milk and home made cheese. Peaches, sugar figs, plums, corn, potatoes and vegetables of all kinds were grown. These along with wild game, sausages, hog's head cheese and sassafras tea all needed to be held, stored and preserved.

Bringing heavy earthenware pottery from Pensacola to Knox Hill and Uchee Anna by flatboat up the Choctawhatchie River or overland by horse drawn wagon had to be tiring and expensive. A local pottery was clearly needed.

Ripley Bullen, a Florida state archeologist, states:

> Turnley (Turnlee) provided the money and the land and Odom was the potter. They were partners. The pottery, was started in 1859 by M.M. Odom and Robert Turnley but was in operation only a little over a year. (6)

Don Fredgant writing in the *Antiques Journal* of 1981 indicates that in the 1930s, Dr. Thompson van Hyning, the then director of the Florida State Museum, traveled through the Florida panhandle collecting specimens of pottery and questioning local residents about the objects he was turning up. He found several specimens of alkaline glazed wares at Knox Hill concentrated near Turnlee Spring, a low, marshy spring formerly in the Turnlee family. Among the pieces he found was one which

A brown salt glazed jug with handle applied directly to the spout and a finger indentation at the base of handle. Height 8 1/4 inches, base 4 3/4 inches, mouth of spout 1 1/4 inches. There is a circumferential indentation about the base. Knox Hill Pottery, Walton County, Florida. Circa 1859-1860. Courtesy Okaloosa Walton Historical Museum. Catalogue number 85:4313.

provided the final link to connect the names of Odom and Turnlee. (7)

The most interesting bears M.M. Odom signed in glaze on one side, the numeral 3 on the other, and an incised line over each handle. It is attractively covered with light green dots. (6) This signed piece is in the collection of the Museum of Florida History. Another impressed block stamped, "T B Odom" is in the collection of the Okaloosa Walton Historical Museum. That the pitcher was impressed

A green black alkaline glazed pitcher. Base of applied handle flattened. Circumferential flare about the base. Base rough and unglazed. Height 9 1/4 inches, base 6 1/8 inches. Mouth 4 3/4 inches. The Knox Hill pottery, Walton County, Florida. Circa 1859-1860. Courtesy Okaloosa Walton Historical Museum.

with a manufactured stamp, whereas the M.M. Odom piece was simply inscribed, suggests that the stamp was to be used for many more pieces. (7)

The Knox Hill pottery produced alkaline glazed stoneware typical of that produced throughout the South. Crocks, pots, churns, pitchers and jugs were all made and can be seen today at the Okaloosa Walton Historical Museum at Valparaiso, Florida and at the Museum of Florida History in Tallahassee.

Ripley Bullen believed that the pottery lasted only one year. That is likely, but at the present time we can't be sure. Why did the pottery close? The Civil War may be the answer. The war cast a cloud over the entire South. Walton County had voted heavily against secession and was briefly called Lincoln County for its pro Lincoln and pro Constitution sentiment, but after Ft. Sumpter, the men of Walton formed the First Florida Regiment and the Sixth Florida Infantry and left their homes to fight for the Confederacy. Pottery, like most commercial interests, was just not important. It is possible that the Odoms and Turnlee enlisted.

After the war, the area slowly began to recover. In 1881 a surveying party for the Louisville and Nashville Railroad planned the town of DeFuniak Springs, where the first Florida Chautauqua was held in 1885. Knox Hill slowly began to dissolve in the memory of following generations as the cultural and civic life of the area revolved around the clear circular lake at DeFuniak.

Today casual inquiries at the local library and the county courthouse as to the location of Knox Hill are met with shrugs, but local historian and retired attorney, Harold Gillis, a descendant of the first Scotch settlers, remembers. An inspection of the Confederate Memorial in front of the Walton County court house reveals that eight Gillis' fought for Walton County. Mr. Gillis' father, John Newton Gillis, was named for the famous teacher at Knox Hill and he, too, remembered the pottery.

The "lost pottery" at Knox Hill is not really lost but simply covered over by time. Harold Gillis gives clear directions to Knox Hill. "Take U.S. 98 east out of DeFuniak Springs to Argyle and at Melhorn's Mini Mart opposite the Argyle Post Office cross the railroad tracks and proceed down that road a few miles until you pass over Interstate 10, make a sharp left turn and you're on Douglass Cross Road. Continue on Douglass Cross Road for a few miles and it becomes Knox Hill Road. Follow this to Crooked Creek and Pursley Hill Roads and you are now at the top of Knox Hill with Pursley Hill to the left and Knox Hill on the right. Further down the road is Rupert Ray Road which runs across the hill." (9)

Today Knox Hill is completely overgrown with a dense cover of palmetto, scrub oak and pine. Wild plants with stickers are everywhere and you have the feeling that there are plenty of rattlesnakes here. At the top of the hill just off the Knox Hill Road are old concrete steps and toppled brick pilings that once provided the foundation for a building. The Knox Hill Academy?

Further on down the hill a dirt road cuts across the hill from Knox Hill Road. An easy walk down this road and you can hear the clear sound of running water. A little further and you come upon a small pond about seventy yards long and thirty wide. The sound of running water comes from an old rusted pipe. Turnlee Spring! The pottery still sits here surrounded by the undergrowth and 140 years of history patiently waiting for Floridians to clear the land and find her again.

A storage jar with lid. Green gray salt glaze on the outside and a light brown salt glaze on the inside. There is a raised turning line below the neck and an incised turning line on the shoulder. Brown black firing marks on body. Circular turning marks on base. Height 7 1/4 inches, width at base 5 1/2 inches. Knox Hill Pottery, Walton County, Florida. Circa 1859-1860. Courtesy Okaloosa Walton Historical Museum. Catalogue number 85:4315.

A red brown salt glazed churn or storage jar with raised turning mark on neck and incised marks on shoulder. Turning marks through body. Circumferential indentation about base. Height 19 3/8 inches, base 8 1/4 inches, mouth 7 1/8 inches. The Knox Hill Pottery, Walton County, Florida. Circa 1859-1860. On display at Okaloosa Walton Historical Museum. Courtesy Museum of Florida History. Catalogue number 62446.

IDENTIFICATION

Early seventeenth century immigrant potters from England and Europe produced the first pottery made in this country. Their kilns were of simple construction and reached low temperatures of 1,000 degrees Celsius. The unglazed and relatively porous pottery produced at these low temperatures is called earthenware. In the early eighteenth century, kilns were better insulated, reaching temperatures of 1,200 degrees Celsius. These kilns produced the salt glazed and alkaline glazed stoneware pottery that was used in the South for food storage. Salt glazing was brought over from Europe but alkaline glazing appears to have originated in the South.

To burn salt ware, unglazed pots are placed in the kiln and when the temperature reaches white heat at 1,225 to 1,260 degrees Celsius, salt is added into the kiln through a hole in the top. The salt vaporizes and the sodium binds with the silica of the clay to form a thin glaze of sodium silicate. The amount of iron in the clay determines the pot's color.

Alkaline glaze is made from ground wood ash mixed with a thin slip of clay. The bisque pottery is dipped in the glaze and then fired . Nancy Sweezy in *Raised in Clay the Southern Pottery Tradition*, states:

> Southern alkaline pots are generally streaked where the glaze has run, a characteristic mark of wood ash when it settles on an unglazed pot in a wood firing....
>
> Alkaline glazes have been fired traditionally with wood in ground hog or railroad tunnel kilns to high temperatures (1,225 to 1,310 degrees Celsius). Since the glazes are frequently runny, the ware is set single level on a sand bed. Various additions or substitutions have been made to the base glaze...black iron sand was added; salt was introduced to lighten the color and lower the maturing temperature of the glaze; crushed glass was used in addition to—or sometimes as a substitute for—wood ash. (10)

Knox Hill Pottery produced alkaline and salt glazed crocks, pots, churns, pitchers and jugs typical of pottery produced in the south. Two signed pots exist. One is stamped, "T B Odom" and the other inscribed "M M Odom." See Fig. 1.

Examination of Knox Hill pottery at the Museum of Florida History in Tallahassee and pottery at the Okaloosa Walton Historical Museum in Valparaiso reveals some common features that will help in identifying unsigned pieces.

Figure 1. M.M. Odom signature on specimen 50309 and T.B. Odom stamp on specimen 73-2311.

HANDLES

Handles on pottery are of two types, a lug handle where four finger tips fit under the handle and a grip handle where the handle is grasped with the encircling thumb and fingers. Four Knox Hill specimens have lug handles with a horizontal groove in the top of the handle. See Fig. 2. Three of the specimens with grip handles (85-4313, 60131, 62433) have one deep fingertip impression at the base of the handle. See Fig. 3. Three other grip handles have tapered ends. (73-2311,85-4314, 62455) See Fig. 4.

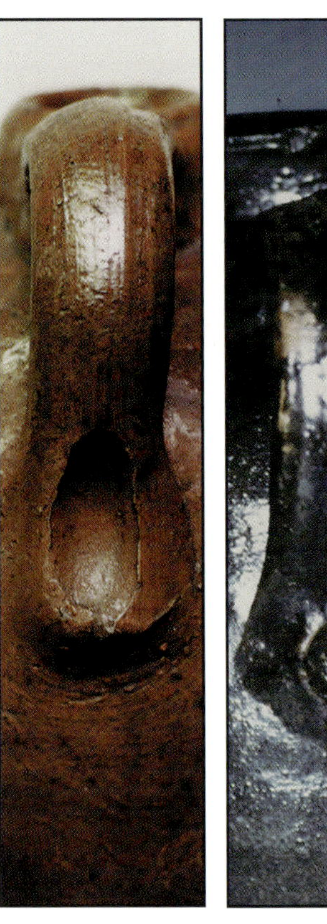

Fig. 3. Finger mark at the base of regular handles. Specimens 62433, 60131 and 85-4313.

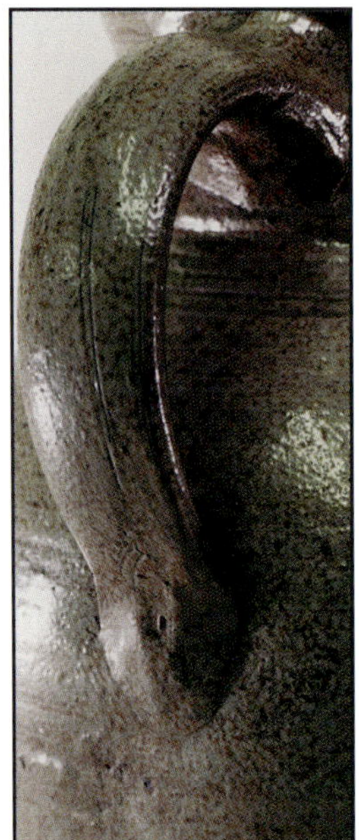
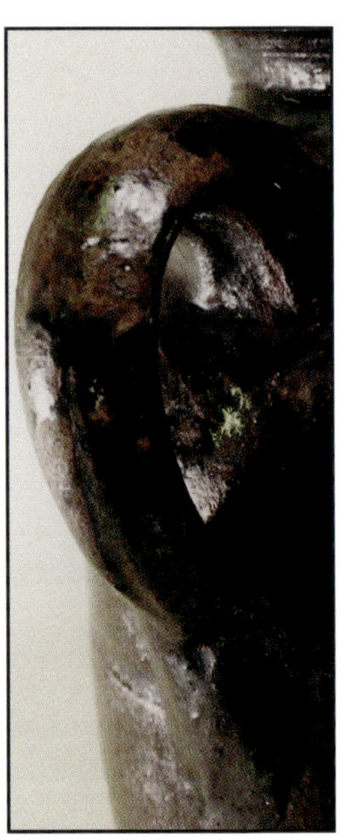

Fig. 4. Three finger smooth handle bases.

Fig. 2. Grooved lug handles on specimens 60124, 50286, and 50309.

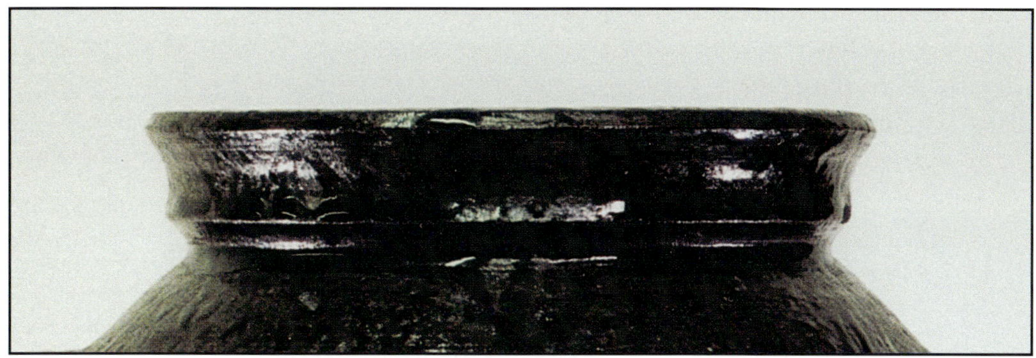

Fig. 5. Crown shape to mouth of specimens 50309, 60124 and 63670.

NUMBERS DENOTING GALLONS

Three of the specimens are marked with numbers indicating the gallon volume of the pot. These numbers appear to be in the same hand. One pot is marked with the impressed "4." See Figure 6.

Fig. 6. Incised gallon numbers 2, 3, 4 and stamped "4."

BASE

Many of the Knox Hill specimens have a characteristic angular shaping to the base. See Figure 7.

Figure 7. Angular shape or indentation found frequently on bases of Knox Hill pottery.

A red brown alkaline glazed stoneware churn, 8 inches in diameter and 13 1/2 inches high, with handle. Knox Hill Pottery, Walton County, Florida. Circa 1859-1860. Courtesy of Museum of Florida History. Catalogue number 62455.

A large unglazed earthware churn with lid and two handles. The handles with pointed rat tail endings. Raised turning on neck and incised on base. Two deep incised lines on lip above handles. Height 16 inches, mouth 8 3/8 inches, base 8 1/2 inches. Marked "4" for 4 gallons. The Knox Hill Pottery, Walton County, Florida. Crica 1859-1860. On display at the Okaloosa Walton Historical Museum from the collection of the Museum of Florida History. Catalogue number 60127.

A dark green-brown glazed stoneware jar with figure "2" incised in the side. Height 12 inches, width 8 1/2 inches. Knox Hill Pottery, Walton County, Florida. Circa 1859-1860. Purchased by T. Van Hyning from a family living near Knox Hill. Courtesy of Museum of Florida History. Catalogue number 63670.

A dark brown alkaline glazed storage jar with black drippings and two applied handles. Handles grooved across the top. Glazed inside and out. Circumferential indentation about the base. Base rough and unglazed. Height 12 1/2 inches, base 6 3/4 inches, mouth 6 5/8 inches. The Knox Hill Pottery, Walton County, Florida. Circa 1859-1860. On display at Okaloosa Walton Historical Museum. Catalogue number 60124. From the collection of Museum of Florida History.

A large brown salt glazed storage jar. Glazed on the outside and partly glazed on the inside. Black firing marks through out the body with a raised turning on the neck and incised circumferential mark on shoulder. Height 15 3/8 inches, width 9 1/8 inches, mouth width 7 7/8 inches. There is a circumferential indentation at the base. Base unglazed red clay. Knox Hill Pottery, Walton County, Florida. Circa 1859-1860. Courtesy Okaloosa Walton Historical Museum. Catalogue number 85: 4312.

A gray green alkaline glazed pot with two handles and turning marks through body. Glazed inside and out. Handles with groove on top. Base rough and unglazed. Height 8 inches, base 6 1/2 inches, mouth 5 7/8 inches. The Knox Hill Pottery, Walton County, Florida. Circa 1859-1860. On display at the Okaloosa Walton Historical Museum from the collection of the Museum of Florida History. Catalogue number 62457.

A brown green alkaline glazed storage jar with two applied handles. Glazed inside and out. Incised line on neck. Turning marks on body. Circumferential line about base with indentation. Handles lightly grooved across top. Rough unglazed base. Height 7 3/8 inches, width 7 1/4 inches. Courtesy Okaloosa Walton Historical Museum. Catalogue number 60125.

Chapter Two

John William Kohler

Southern Pottery Works
Pensacola, Florida
1869-1908

The first successful commercial pottery in the State of Florida was started by John William Kohler in Pensacola in 1869.

John H. Kohler, one of the four sons of John William Kohler described his father:

John William Kohler was born in Buffalo, New York in the year 1837 and was reared in and around Detroit, Michigan until he was about sixteen years old. While he was on a trip over in Missouri the 'Pike's Peak Gold Mine Rush' was in its height, and he and some other relatives and friends joined the 'ox cart train' and made the trip all the way from Omaha, Nebraska to Pike's Peak in an ox cart. Anyone who has read the story of 'The Covered Wagon' can appreciate about what they went through with, as his stories to us children related many years afterwards were almost identical with this one.

Soon after returning from this long, tedious trip, the war between the North and South was declared, and while he was a northern born man, his sympathies were always with the South and, rather than go to war against the South, he moved to Nashville, Tennessee and stayed there all during the war. Immediately after the war he came south again and went to work in the Pensacola Navy Yard, building wooden ships and other government materials.

Many times he related how they would take the oak logs out of Commodore's

A flower pot 15 inches diameter and 13 1/2 inches high, of light yellow earthenware with two applied handles and the face of a lady. Made by J. W. Kohler, Pensacola, Florida. Circa 1869-1908. Courtesy Museum of Florida History. Catalogue number 50313.

Pond, which is only a little distance this side of the Navy Yard wall, and many of these logs can be seen in this pond even to this day.

While working at the Navy Yard, he became acquainted with my mother, who was the daughter of Captain Silas Lawrence, who, at that time, was keeper of the lighthouse and they were married and went to housekeeping for themselves. Soon afterwards Captain Lawrence was given full control of all live oak reserves in the United States and moved his family to what is called "The Live Oak Reserves" in Santa Rosa County on the Peninsula opposite where the Quarantine Station is now located, and while they were living at this place my father began his first pottery in the South. However, he had been raised in the pottery business, as his father and grandfather were both potters.

In those days he carried the clay in boats from some point along the Escambia Bay on the Pensacola side and made up the pottery at the Live Oak Reserve, but in after years, sometime about 1870, he came over to the Pensacola side and bought property on East Hill, known as New City, and there conducted his pottery for at least forty years, having found a good clay bed that lasted him the entire length of time. At this place most of the children were born and reared. (1)

One of a set of four food safe saucers. These saucers were filled with kerosene and placed under the feet of food safes to protect food from insects. Southern Pottery Works, Pensacola, Florida. John W. Kohler, potter. Circa 1869-1908. Courtesy, Pensacola Historical Society.

John Kohler ran this advertisment in "Bliss Quarterly," January 1897, Vol. III, No. 3, and notes that the Southern Pottery Works was established in 1869.

A jar 8 1/2 inches in diameter and 9 inches high, of light yellow earthenware. From Southern Pottery Works, Pensacola, Florida. John W. Kohler, potter. Circa 1869-1908. Courtesy Museum of Florida History. Catalogue number 50323.

A flower pot 4 1/2 inches diameter and 4 inches high of light yellow earthenware. Made by John W. Kohler, Southern Pottery Works, Pensacola, Florida. Circa 1869-1908. Courtesy Museum of Florida History. Catalogue number 50317.

An advertisement in Pensacola's *Bliss Quarterly* indicates the Kohler pottery was actually started in 1869. (2) The Pensacola City Directories indicate that both the Southern Pottery Works and the Kohler residence were located at the north end of 8th Avenue from, at the latest, 1885 through to 1903. It's likely that the pottery began in Pensacola at the 8th Avenue location and remained there until 1903 or 1904. In 1905 the City Directory finds the Southern Pottery Works located at 818 East Moreno Street and the family residence next door at 816 East Moreno.

A story in the editorial section of the *Pensacola Commercial* on November 3, 1882 gave the first public notice of the pottery.

A Reporter's Ride - Kohler Pottery - Tar, Pitch and Turpentine, etc. We stood at the corner of Merchants' Hotel on Wednesday, looking up and down for some interesting item. We were suddenly tapped on the shoulder by Mr. J.G. Woods, the gentlemanly hackman, who instinctively read our thoughtful desire and said, "Jump in, sir, my horses are at your disposal."

We did jump in and gladly too, for we knew we would ride behind such horse flesh as would ever make man proud. "Where?" asked Mr. Woods. "To the Kohler's Pottery," said we, and the horses galloped at a lively pace and we soon were riding up Palaflox Street but were terribly jostled by reason of the uneven, undulating road. Now ye City Fathers or those in charge, level this street, pound down the rock, and as Mr. Woods said, "ten dollars will do the work."

Passing this road, we rode on, and soon came in sight of Kohler's Pottery. Mr. Kohler noticing our modesty, begged us to enter his premises and Mr. Woods and the writer will recount what they heard and saw, as briefly as possible.

Eight years ago Mr. Kohler, coming from Detroit, Michigan, where he "shaped" his trade, came to Pensacola and saw an opening to that occupation which has since established him as a man of foresight and energy; he found here rich clay capable of the richest pottery ware. If our readers recollect that there is no other pottery, in Florida, that none other, as far as we know, had ever been worked here, they will at once appreciate the hardship of such a new enterprise. But Mr. Kohler did not despair of ultimate success and a mile from the city has, year by year, built his trade - and is known throughout the Southern country.

We gazed, and wondered and asked: "How is it so few have invested in this occupation?" and Mr. Kohler at once let in the light by telling how much Northern labor is paid for some of the work and that the scarcity of labor in the South, interferes in a great measure with its prosperity.

After showing us through the entire buildings, about 3 in number, molds

An urn 11 inches in diameter and 17 inches high, of light yellow earthenware. From Southern Pottery Works, Pensacola, Florida. Circa1869-1908. John W. Kohler, potter. Courtesy Museum of Florida History. Catalogue number 50322.

originally manufactured from the clay in the yard, vases of every conceivable shape and size; piping ready for Mobile orders, butter pots to be sent to New Orleans, all kinds of terra cotta work, all these demonstrated more than words can tell, the success of this business.

Mr. Kohler then practically showed us the mechanism of all this. He took about a pound of gray clay, all of which is dug on the premises, kneaded it, shaped it on a revolving block, which is moved by the left foot, turned to us and asked "What will you have?" Here the clay in the potter's hand, before our eyes and those of Mr. Woods, stopped wondering, we saw a jar, then a spittoon, then a vase, then a flower pot, butter pot and all kinds of earthen ware made in our presence - all done in less than a minute. Thanking Mr. Kohler for what he had taught us, we bade a hasty adieu, for fear of troubling him longer and we returned to town. (3)

The Pensacola Directories of 1890-1891 and 1893-1894 gave a good description of the pottery produced by John Kohler, "Manufacturer of Stone and Earthenware, milk pans, stew pans, chicken fountains, safe saucers, flower pots, ornamental and plain hanging baskets, vases for fountains, for garden and cemetery use, window pots, etc. Antique pots made to order, ornamental and plain chimney tops, all sizes of drain and sewer pipes."

From 1869 to 1908 the Pensacola Pottery Works produced stoneware needed to survive in Florida. The advent of mass produced containers such as the Mason jar, tinware and graniteware along with the South slowly changing from an agrarian to a market economy, forced Kohler and other early Southern rural potters out of business. Kohler's advancing age was also a factor.

About 1908 Kohler moved to Central Florida, probably to St. Petersburg, where he lived with his son Joseph A. Kohler. John W. Kohler returned to Pensacola shortly before his death on March 15, 1915.

The *Pensacola Journal* carried his obituary.

J.W. KOHLER DIES AFTER LONG ILLNESS PASSES AWAY AT HIS HOME CORNER FOURTEENTH STREET AND NINTH AVENUE AT AGE OF 79 YEARS.

J.W. Kohler, one of the oldest citizens of Pensacola, died last night at 8:45 o'clock at his home, corner Fourteenth Street and Ninth Avenue. Death was due to advanced age and complications.

Mr. Kohler, until eight or nine years ago, when he went to South Florida, had lived in Pensacola practically all his life.

A flower pot 13 1/2 inches diameter and 9 inches high, of light yellow earthenware. Made by John W. Kohler, Southern Pottery Works, Pensacola, Florida. Circa 1869-1908. Courtesy Museum of Florida History. Catalogue number 50319.

He remained in South Florida until a few weeks ago, when he returned here with his family. (4)

John William Kohler is buried in Pensacola's St. Johns Cemetery. He, like George Ohr, "The Mad Potter of Biloxie," was one of the first to spend most of his adult life producing pottery for the southern market. His legacy of work remains scattered, undiscovered, throughout the South. His son, Joseph A. Kohler, would continue the family tradition of pottery making in St. Petersburg, Florida.

IDENTIFICATION

There are 19 specimens attributed to the Kohler pottery in the collection of the Museum Of Florida History in Tallahassee. All are unglazed. Four Albany slip glazed food safe saucers are in the collection of the Pensacola Historical Society. Don Fredgant indicates that other glazed examples have survived and that one signed piece exists in a private collection.

Fredgant states:

Unfortunately, attributions to the Kohler Pottery...are difficult for several reasons. First, there is a scarcity of pieces in the Pensacola area with the right "feel" of the Kohler pieces. Second, only a single signed piece is known to be in a collection, making signed specimens truly rare. Third, although J.W. Kohler's pottery was the most successful commercial pottery in Florida's history, it faced competition with similar products made in Southern Alabama, some of which are now mistaken for Pensacola pieces.

The only "signed" piece of pottery known from the Kohler pottery is in the collection of a private Florida collector. It is a stoneware storage jar or small churn with a dark brown glaze, standing about 15 inches high. The three-line impressed mark at the shoulder read: J.W.KOHLER/ PENSACOLA/ FLORIDA.

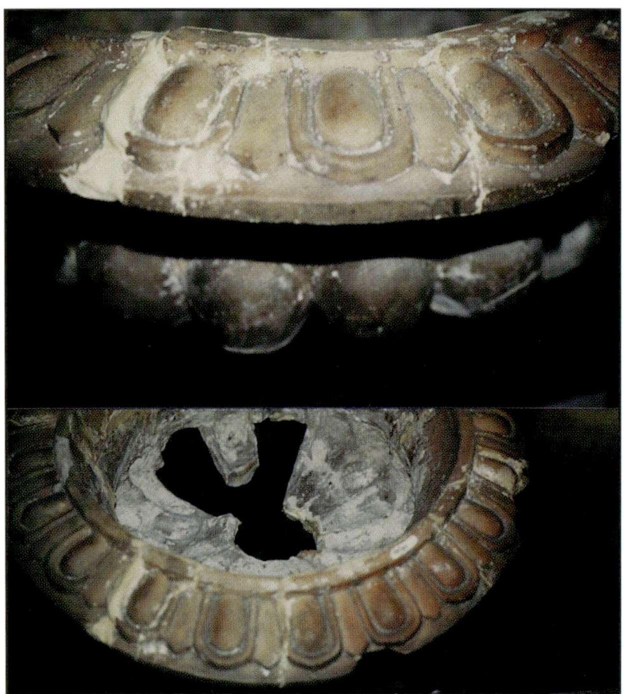

A large earthernware bowl or urn (broken with losses). Southern Pottery Works, Pensacola, Florida. Circa 1869-1908. Courtesy, Museum of Florida History. Catalogue number 50383.

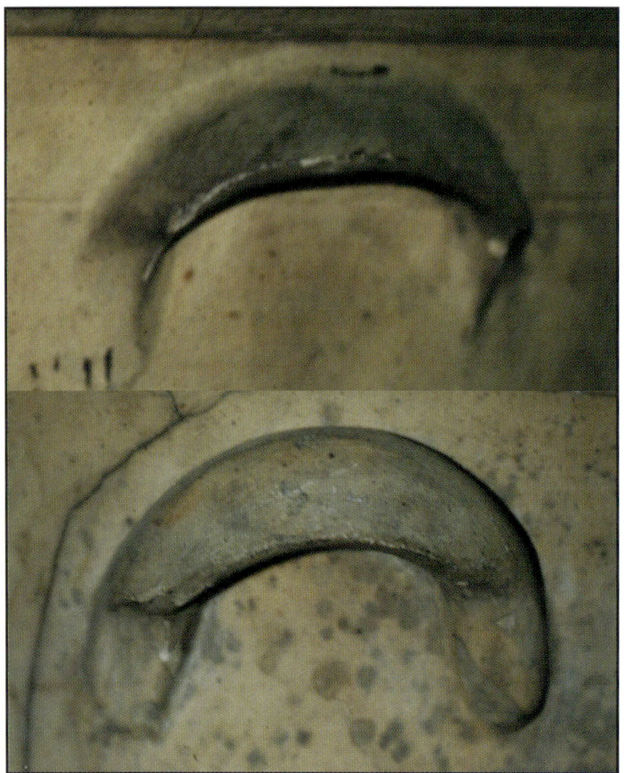

Two lug handles applied to the sides of earthernware pots catalogue number 50313 and 50319. Note the ends of the handles are flattened, in one flush with the pot and the other nearly flush. The lower inner edge of 50316 is sharp.

The bases of two Southern Pottery Works flower pots showing drainage holes and grooves cut in the base to permit easy drainage.

Most pieces attributed locally to Kohler are of terra cotta, ranging from a pale tan or buff to reddish brown. Most of the production was in such utilitarian items as flower pots, jugs, (occasionally "stuccoed," as one relative remembers, with pieces of coins, tokens or metal) and drain pipe. (5)

Kohler made wheel thrown and press molded pottery as found in the partly restored earthenware urn in the Museum of Florida History collection. Presence of a Kohler molded face on a specimen remains, aside from a signed piece, the only presently reliable method of identification.

Molded decorative figures from the Southern Pottery Works used to ornament pottery. Courtesy Museum of Florida History.

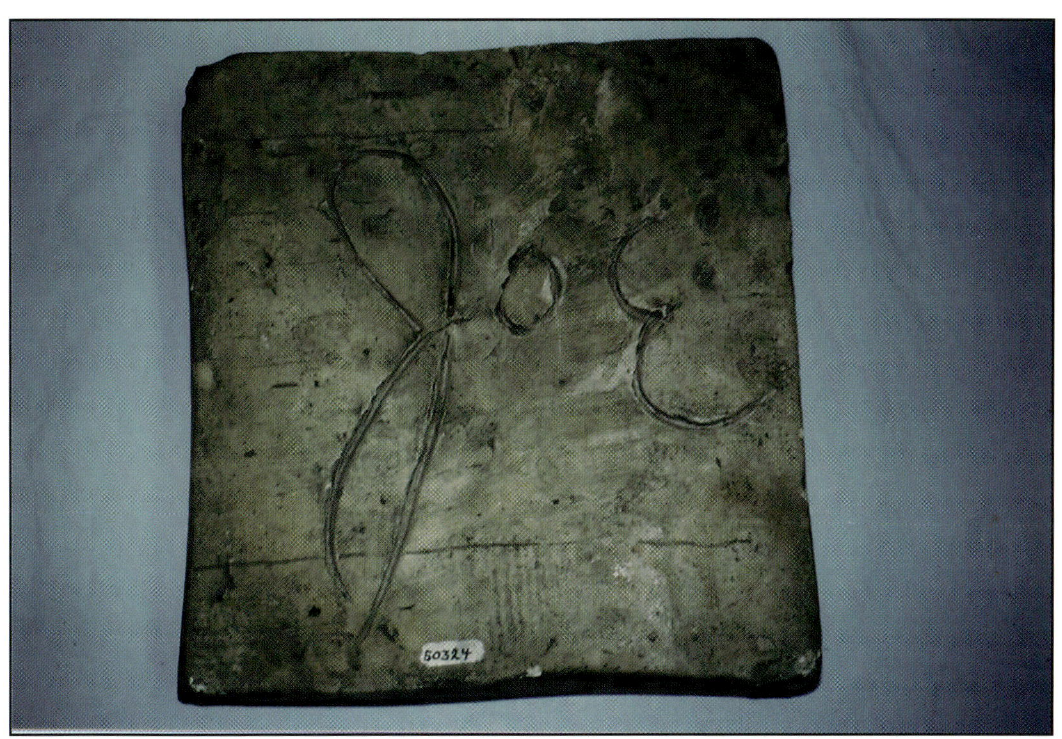

An unglazed earthenware tablet with "Joe" inscribed. Perhaps signed by John Kohler's son, Joseph Kohler. Years later Joe Kohler would open his own pottery in St. Petersburg, Florida. Courtesy Museum of Florida History.

Chapter Three

Henry F. York, Captain 7th Florida Infantry, CSA. Founder of the York Pottery, Lake Butler, Florida. Circa 1888. Picture courtesy Mrs. Hal York Maines, Lake Butler, Florida

York Pottery
Lake Butler, Florida
1888-1890

In 1872 a thirty-eight year old Confederate veteran of the Civil War, Captain Henry F. York, built a Victorian revival house at 180 South Lake Avenue in Lake Butler, Florida. York built the house from hand planed pine boards that were milled on the clearing site. The two large chimneys and foundation pillars of the house were made of brick, hand made from clay dug on the property. These yellow bricks served not just as the foundation of York's house but represented his first attempts to bake clay into useful objects. Years later York got the idea for a pottery. (1)

The search for the "Lost Pottery" of Lake Butler begins in a quiet rural cemetery some thirty miles north of Gainesville. On a warm summer evening the approach to the Old Providence Baptist Church Cemetery off Route 238 in western Union County is broken only by an occasional bird and the hum of a passing car. Walking between the grave markers looking for Henry York's grave the sand spurs will bite your legs as if the surrounding dead don't want to be disturbed. Finding the grave, a recent headstone indicates the family is still looking after the old gent. Here is Captain York, the founder of the York Pottery and his wife, Salome Sasser. (2)

Henry York was born in Franklin County, Georgia on November 11, 1834. He moved to the Lake Butler area well before the onset of the Civil War. In April of 1862, York along with many young men from the area, were mustered into the Confederate Army as Company "A" of the 7th Florida Infantry. York was elected Captain. (3)

York and the 7th Florida regiment were sent west where they served briefly with General Kirby Smith. In September of 1863, York and the Florida regiments joined with General Bragg's army and served with heroism at Chickamauga and

A small cream pitcher 5 inches high and 3 1/2 inches at the base. Press molded stoneware with light yellow glaze. Decorated with a basketweave caneware pattern on the body, bands encircling the neck and base and a branch like handle. Marked and inscribed with a crude "Y or X." Maines family collection, Lake Butler, Florida.

Missionary Ridge. At Missionary Ridge a picket force of the Florida First dismounted and the Fourth regiments were sent forth to engage the enemy. General Gates described the action.

The pressure of the enemy on our front, on the morning of the 25th, forbade the relief of this force. By repeated application from the front I was induced to send the 7th Florida as a reserve to our picketline. This little force (with Captain York leading "A" Company) under the frown of such horrid front remained defiant, and in obedience to orders maneuvered handsomely amid the peril of capture until, by order, it found a lodgment in the trenches at the foot of Missionary Ridge, with its right resting at

Moore's house. I ordered that it hold the trenches at all hazards. (4)

An overwhelming force of Union soldiers forced the Confederate troops out of their entrenchment's and back up Missionary Ridge, where exposed to continuous fire they were killed, wounded or captured. The troops in the trenches and those on the summit all fought gallantly. General Gates reported the loss of his division at 43 killed, 224 wounded, missing 590, and added, "Most of the latter were Floridians who were in the trenches." Henry York took a Minnie ball through the left chest. Mrs. Hal Maines, the wife of Henry York's grandson, tells the following story.

Two Yankees came upon York lying on the field and were about to kill him. York, a Mason, gave the sign of a Mason in distress. The Yankees didn't shoot. A silk handkerchief was used to plug the wound and Henry York was taken prisoner. (5)

At the war's end York was released and returned to Lake Butler where he was a partner in the York & Rhodes general stores. York & Rhodes was a typical general store of the times. They kept a barrel of liquor in a side room and sold it to customers who brought their own jugs. York later became the first Clerk of the Court for what was then Bradford County and served in that capacity from 1877 to 1889. (6)

A teapot with lid. 5 inches high 8 inches wide and 31/2 inches at base. Press molded stoneware with light yellow glaze. Decorated with an orange peel effect on the body, spout and lid, flowers and leaves on the body, leaves on lid and spout and a tree branch like handle. Marked "FLORIDA" on the base. Maines family collection, Lake Butler, Florida.

Starke became the Bradford County seat in 1887. A review of the *Starke Telegraph* from 1886 to 1888, when the paper became the *Bradford County Telegraph,* reveals that York, as Clerk of the County Court, was a busy man involved daily in the business of the court and traveling between Lake Butler and Starke.

The *Starke Telegraph* of April 6, 1888 contains the first notice of plans for a pottery in Lake Butler.

William Greig of Scotland arrived here Monday and left at once for Lake Butler, where he takes charge of the pottery

---

works of York and Craig. It is expected that this stoneware factory will soon be in full operation.

Ripley Bullen, a Florida state archeologist, writing in 1970 states,

Another pottery was started by H.F. York at Lake Butler, Union County, Florida in 1884. Having successfully fired bricks for house supports, chimneys and fireplaces, he decided, after receiving advice from a Mr. Craig of Atlanta, 'an expert potter from Scotland', to attempt the manufacture of pottery vessels. He engaged Will Gregg, 'another expert from Scotland,' who supervised the

---

A water pitcher 8 1/4 inches high and 5 1/2 inches at base. Fish scale-like decoration on the body and flower medallions on sides. Press molded stoneware with blue glaze. Marked with a "Y" on base. Maines family collection, Lake Butler, Florida.

A water pitcher 9 3/4 inches high and 7 inches wide. Press molded stoneware with blue glaze. Decorated with banding at neck and base and cows in medallion on sides. Marked with a "Y" on base. Maines family collection, Lake Butler, Florida.

building of a 'great Down Draft pottery kiln', and the making of many large saggars. Also provided was machinery to liquefy, screen, and then evaporate or dry the clay. This operation was a major undertaking and the kiln alone is said to have cost $1,500. (7)

Bullen was incorrect in his starting date of 1884. The *Bradford County Telegraph* of June 29, 1888 announced,

> The Lake Butler pottery works will soon be under way and will turn out earth-enware for all the country.

In the August 10th issue a local correspondent "with some interest and pleasure" states regarding Lake Butler,

> We have a telephone, a pottery, four stores, a fine day school and also a writing class.

Clearly by August of 1888 the people of Lake Butler recognized they had a local pottery.

It wasn't until nearly a year later, on May 17, 1889, that the first advertisements of pottery for sale appeared in the Bradford paper.

> You can buy all the stone jugs, etc. etc. you want from Capt. H.F. York of Lake Butler but if there is anything else you need call at J.G. Alvarez and get it.

This ad appeared in the next three issues of the *Telegraph* and on June 21 the paper announced,

> "Capt. York has his first kiln of pottery ware burned. It is the best ever made. There is no doubt but Captain York has a fortune in his clay works. (9)

In July the *Telegraph* ran the following article.

> BRADFORD AHEAD…Capt. H.F. York of Lake Butler, had on exhibition in this city one day last week, a sample of his pottery ware taken from his first kiln. The samples were all pitchers of a most difficult and delicate design. They were perfectly made and as handsome and light as clay ware of its kind ever brought to our notice. Capt. York has an inexhaustible supply of clay for pottery. This is the only bed of kaolin in the Southern states and the best in the United States. Capt. York gave the credit of the discovery of this bed of clay entirely to Prof. F.G. Shell, who made the discovery and called the Captain's attention to his fortune some three years or more ago. Prof. Shell is one of the best chemists in the state and a valuable citizen. He has other discoveries of great value yet to be developed. Capt. York has at great expense erected a suitable kiln and other arrangements for the manufacture of all kinds of pottery, which he proposes to do on a large scale. The new Macon railroad will pass within a few rods of the works, thus making transportation easy. This infant industry should have all the assistance needful by our country as well as the state in general. It will bring capital into Bradford and the state. (10)

A plate or shallow bowl 9 inches wide and 1 1/2 inches high. Decorated with leaflike edges, green alligator skin borders and green leaf at center. Press molded stoneware with clear glaze. Unmarked. Maines family collection, Lake Butler, Florida.

Ripley Bullen goes on to state,

> This initial firing produced an amazing assortment of jars, jugs, churns, bowls, pitchers, flower pots and cuspidors including — if our records are correct — two part mold made pitchers with roses, leaves and stems in low relief on each side. Made of a gray bodied stoneware, one has a thin yellow-brown glaze on both inner and outer surfaces. The other exhibits a clear yellow glaze with underglaze red and green painting which, in places, ran. The glaze on these containers is not salt glaze. It has a high reflecting power like alkaline glaze but I do not know the type of glaze used. Clearly these were experimental pieces and the glaze material may have been imported from Georgia or further north. (11)

Henry York had built his pottery with a clear eye on the new railroad coming to town. The Georgia Southern and Florida Railroad had completed their track into Lake Butler in November of 1889 and by December 200 boxes of oranges and 200 bales of cotton were shipped out. For some reason that may never be known, York was unable to market his stoneware pottery "for all the country."

Captain York had been seriously wounded at Missionary Ridge but his health must have been excellent as evidenced by his willingness, at age 53, to risk considerable capital on the development of a pottery. Pottery sales in large volume never materialized and in March of 1890 York began plans to go into the brick business. Unexpectedly, Henry York died on July 2, 1890. His obituary reads:

> Died at his home at Lake Butler, Wednesday, July 2nd, Capt. Henry F. York, in the fifty-sixth year of his age. Henry F. York was born at Franklin County, Georgia in 1834. In 1857 he moved to Bradford County, Florida where he ever since lived. The first two years he taught school near Providence. In 1858 he engaged in the mercantile business at Lake Butler and soon after married Miss Sassier, his surviving widow. In 1859 he was elected to the Office of the Clerk of the Circuit Court, which office he filled until the war broke out, when he resigned his position and went into the war as first lieutenant of a Bradford County company. He was soon promoted to Captain of the company. He was wounded by a Minnie ball passing through his body just above the left nipple, at the battle of Missionary Ridge, Tennessee. He was then captured and taken to Johnson's Island, where he was confined until the close of the war, when he returned to Lake Butler and again engaged in mercantile business at that place. In 1866 he was again elected Clerk of the Circuit Court, which office he filled until removed by the Harrison Reed Administration on account of politics. He was again appointed Clerk of the Circuit Court under the Drew Administration in 1876, and held the office continuously until 1889. He was an active politician and chairman of the county Democratic executive committee of this county from the close of the war until 1884. Capt. York was a lifelong member of the Missionary Baptist Church, a Royal Arch Mason of good standing and a man of great ability. He had many friends and but few enemies. He leaves a wife and three children. His remains were buried in Olustee Cemetery on Thursday last. (12)

Henry York survived a Minnie ball through the chest at Missionary Ridge. His life had been, as Justice Holmes noted, "touched by fire."

The same fire that burned in him as a youth, drove him to build a great down draft kiln and the third pottery in Florida. If York had lived the pottery might be famous. Today, Floridians can take pride in the efforts of this gallant Confederate.

IDENTIFICATION

Henry York produced two different types of pottery, wheel thrown redware; and press molded salt-glazed stoneware.

Two traditional wheel thrown, unglazed storage jars are in the collection of the Museum of Florida History in Tallahassee along with an unglazed mixing bowl with an interior Albany slip glaze.

The York-Maines family has a number of salt glazed press molded examples that have passed down in the family including a teapot, two blue and white pitchers, a small cream pitcher and a plate.

Salt glazed press molded stoneware began to be produced in this country in the mid 1800s and the "milking cow" and the "fishscale and wild rose" pitchers were common patterns produced by several manufacturers during the golden era of molded stoneware from 1890 to the mid 1930s. (13) (14) These manufacturers and York may have purchased their molds from the same supplier. Marked examples of blue stoneware are uncommon but the two blue pitchers in the York-Maines collection are both marked with a cobalt blue "Y." The yellow cream pitcher is also marked with a "Y" in green and an incised "X" or "Y." The presence of a blue "Y" on the base of a molded piece of stoneware may be a reliable sign of York Pottery work but more study is needed. The teapot marked with a hand scripted *Florida* is the only known piece so marked.

The "Y" or "X" mark on the base of cream pitchers.

The "Y" on the base of blue pitchers.

Chapter Four

Mary Ward, Manatee River Pottery.
Circa 1920

Manatee River Pottery
Bradentown, Florida
1915-1921

Mary Herrick Ward, born in Tennessee, was a 28 year-old red-headed divorcee and a mother of two when she moved to Bradentown from New York City in 1914. Given the social and religious attitudes of the time one can almost hear the gossip of the ladies of the town. Mary, along with her children Helen and Jimmy, moved into a small cottage at 805 Manatee Ave. three houses east of 26th St. (1)

Where Mrs. Ward received her training in pottery making may never be known, but subsequent events clearly indicate she had significant training in pottery production. An active, intelligent woman, it wasn't long before she was looking for an outlet for her creative energy.

The first public notice of Mary Ward and her pottery appeared in an August issue of the *Manatee River Evening Journal (MRJ)*.

ART CLASS IN SECOND EXHIBIT SHINE BRIGHTLY

Manatee Valley Pottery is Added Feature in Display of Unique Souvenirs

The second exhibit by Mrs. Joseph's art class is in progress at the studio in the New Wallace Theater block today. An interesting feature has been added in the pottery exhibit modeled by a class organized since Mrs. Herrick Ward and Mrs. Joseph began the work of manufacture of unique pottery from the Manatee clay they discovered, and for which exceptional merit is claimed. The class, which comprises Mrs. Fell, Mrs. Spring, Miss Armstrong and Gladys Joseph has made remarkable progress. Many pieces of the pretty pottery are among the exhibits.

Among the art exhibits is a full dinner set, occupying a large table, done by Mrs. Nettie Herrin in small roses. The most attractive of the pieces by Mrs. Herrin is a handsome tankard in peaches. Miss Blanche Alderman exhibits a dinner set of 78 pieces in pale pink roses. The studio in the New Wallace building is splendidly lighted and gives opportunity for favorable display of the exhibit. Criticism of the public is invited and large numbers have visited. (2)

For some reason the paper had called the Manatee River Pottery the "Manatee VALLEY Pottery," but that would be corrected shortly.

In November the *MRJ* carried the following announcement,

The formal opening of the Manatee River Pottery under the direction of Mrs. Herrick Ward, will be held Friday and Saturday, November 19th and 20th, at the pottery, corner of Manatee and Sarasota avenues. The operation of the potter's wheel will be one of the attractions. A tea room, known as the Koffee Klatch, making a specialty of German coffee cake will be opened in the same building by Mrs. C.C. Brooks. On Friday Mrs. Brooks will serve for the benefit of the Women's Club and on Saturday for the State Orphanage. (3)

The new year brought with it the South Florida Fair, held on the fair grounds of the city park. Antique quilts, samplers and wedding gowns fashioned by the fingers of pioneers, and relics of the days of the Seminoles in Manatee County were among the exhibits. When the fair opened on February 13, 1916, Manatee River Pottery was one of the exhibits.

In 1969, Mrs. Lawrence Dowd, of Bradenton, delivered the following detailed talk on the history of the Manatee River Pottery.

It's good to be here, I hope my voice holds out.... My remarks...will be centered about the Manatee River (Pottery), beginning sometime around the turn of the century. I'm not going to date it exactly. I have asked many people for information but the earliest I got was from Louise Wadham Fuller.... When she was a little girl her father was superintendent of Fuller's Earth Works just north of Ellenton.... They found a beautiful blue clay along the river which they were able to work up and put into shape. The sun dried it and then with the aid of an old wood stove it was quite durable for what they wanted it. It was good enough for the time, but their interest changed from mud pies but they will appear later in my story.

However, Fuller's Earth continued as quite an industry. That deposit up the river was owned by the Standard Oil Company and the colored men who worked there had to wear masks to dig the earth from the pit. Then it was loaded on flat cars, sent down to the river where boats from Tampa and St. Pete picked it up. It started on the way to Philadelphia where it was used to refine oil. In Bible times, Fuller's Earth was used to remove oil and dirt from wool. But the oil company reversed it. Then they tried to make Fuller's Earth into talcum powder but it didn't work. The boys who lived around here and who learned to swim in the old swimming hole in Ware's Creek remember the soap stone deposit by the alligator hole. They would break off pieces and work them into a good lather. They also found clay good enough to make marbles. But the girls were thinking in terms of dishes and mud pies....

In the fall of 1916, my sister Ruby came here as the bride of Marshall Coarsey.... It was soon after that she began writing about a Mrs. Ward who had come to Bradentown and was making pottery. She was a very industrious person and she was her neighbor. Mrs. Ward was living in the Wilhemsen house, second house from 26th and on the north side of Manatee Avenue. Soon Ruby was sending us gifts of candlesticks, vases and small items which Mrs. Ward had made....

The pottery business was not that easy for Mrs. Ward. She had come from New York with her two children in 1914 and started the pottery in 1915. She had to find the right clay deposit first... and she went over every bit of property there looking for clay. It was just not there. So she hunted up and down the river and then found a good deposit closer to home than she expected in the 2700 block of Riverview Blvd. Most of the work done to refine the clay was soon done by a man from Ohio, but it was a Mr. Bogsdall who gathered it and it was Fogarty's Dray that brought it to the pottery. In the rear of the house were three rooms, one after the other.

One had the wheels used for making the pottery, but there was one wheel run by electric power. The others were worked by foot power. From all the things I have been told about Mrs. Ward, I think she was a very strong, exceptional character. She was little, thin, wiry and above all a redhead....

She had two children, Helen and Jimmy, who was a real boy. A few blocks away lived two of his buddies, but in between was the Harris dairy. The boys played around at one thing and another and then discovered they could chase the cows and even got to milking them.

Finally, Mrs. Harris discovered that they were short of milk, so she began to watch and discovered just what she expected. Mrs. Harris made two calls, first to the mother of the two boys, and the mother's reply was that she was so sorry. Next went a call to Mrs. Ward and her response was: 'Measure the milk and let me know how much you lack.' That was just what Mrs. Harris did. When Jimmy came home, his mother confronted him with the situation and said that all good sports pay for their fun. He did just that and thus ends the saga of the afternoon milking.

Mrs. Ward shaped every piece of the pottery on a foot treadle wheel and then fired it at a very low temperature. But then she needed help with the decoration and the artwork. Bradentown has always had artists and one of the outstanding ones with pottery was Miss Carrie Phillips. Her name began appearing on the Ward products and we had several pieces that had her name on them. All of a sudden it was Caroline Phillips....There were beautiful products, candlesticks with little Florida scenes. This does not have a Florida scene but they were peacock minded at the time.... That is the natural color of all the clay which came out of the river. It was blue to begin with and turned that color on being fired. They painted lovely Florida scenes..you'd have a beautiful palm tree with palmettos at the bottom..there was always some water..a puddle of water and Florida birds were flying there. Ash trays would be painted and she got to making tall things…table lamp bases.

Miss Denise Shields used to do most of the waterproofing. Now these were never glazed. They put a waterproof mixture of varnish and paint on..nothing

A vase decorated with cormorants flying over bamboo, 4 inches wide and 13 1/2 inches high. Signed, "O. M. Copson." Unmarked. Attributed to Manatee River Pottery, Bradentown, Florida. Circa 1915-1921. Courtesy Manatee County Historical Society.

more..it was fired only one time. The mixture was put on after it was fired..nothing on the outside except the decoration. Consequently, it was not durable and you don't do much cleaning on it. Maybe that's why some folks threw it out. They couldn't get a high enough temperature with their kerosene kilns to put glaze on, so they have smeared and faded....

Display shelves of the Manatee River Pottery and later the Graack Pottery at Bradentown, Florida. Circa 1915-1923. Photograph courtesy of the Manatee County Historical Society.

The name Bob Elliott kept coming up as I talked to several people and I was amazed that he was the same one who finished high school in the early twenties. He must have begun painting for Mrs. Ward when he was 11 or 12 years old. He did quantities of painting in oils as well as watercolors....

There was Miss Mildred Bollinger who came here from Indiana.... She came down to visit Mrs. Pierson in 1916 and she was here for two years. She helped Mrs. Ward in the pottery. She wrote Mrs. Pierson recently, recalling an English artist who came and worked at the pottery. His name was Mr. Coxson. He did work on the large pieces. Another of our local talent who worked at the pottery

A nut dish decorated with pine cones. 6 1/2 inches wide and 1 1/2 inches high. Unmarked. Attributed to the Manatee River Pottery, Bradentown, Florida. Circa 1915-1921.

with Miss Bollinger was Frances Riggins and they both went to St. Pete in 1918. Then there was a real artist who came from England by the name of Mr. Ireland.... He added a great deal to the business....

One art leads to another and before long the pottery business grew to include all kinds of Florida novelties. The business expanded so they moved downtown to Fourth Avenue. They were making sun bonnets they made out of palmetto fans....There were lovely handbraided hats. I wore one Mable made and they were made from the tender parts of the palmetto. They made dolls, and pine needle work, brushes from the Palmetto roots. How those go with pottery I don't know. Then they began filling the bowls with candied grapefruit peel which was a novelty then. The building was a two story one, off Tenth Street. The lower floor was used for the wheels and the kiln and the showroom was on the second floor. Several young people were employed. I asked one if they were paid by the piece or by the hour. The reply was: By the piece, and sometime not.... With business growing Mrs. Ward was packing things in excelsior.... She was shipping to St. Petersburg and New York and several other places.

One young fellow, when he was in high school, applied for a job and he wanted to paint nudes. But was turned down. Too bad he was 50 years too soon.... (4)

During the summer of 1916 the pottery was open on Tuesday and Thursday afternoons.(5) Mrs.Ward spent the summer in Clarksville, Georgia and returned to her home in Bradentown for the winter season on October 1, 1916. (6)

In January The Manatee River Pottery has some of its 1917 work on exhibition on the upper floor

A large vase decorated with Florida dunes and hunting dogs. Unmarked. Attributed to Manatee River Pottery, Bradentown, Florida. Circa 1915-1921.

A wall sconce decorated with daisies, 9 1/2 inches high and 3 inches wide. Unmarked. Attributed to Manatee River Pottery, Bradentown, Florida. Circa 1915-1921.

of the New Wallace Theater building and the *MRJ* noted that the pottery was now baked to a temperature of 1,500 degrees making it impervious to water. (7) Money had clearly become available to purchase a new kiln.

Mrs. Ward lived next door to S. A. Bean, an attorney. Her friendship with Mr. Bean, and exposure of her pottery at the New Wallace theater and the Florida State Fair must have gotten the attention of the leaders of the city. Just after Christmas of 1917 the MRJ ran the following announcement on the front page.

MANATEE RIVER POTTERY WAS
GRANTED A CHARTER
Among charters granted by the Secretary of State during the week is one to the Manatee River Pottery of this city. It is authorized to manufacture and sell pottery, earthenware, tiling and similar articles and has a capital stock of $10,000. The officers are: H.S. Glazier, president; E.P. Hubbell, vice president; S.A. Bean, secretary;   Katherine E. McClellan,

A flower bowl with center frog decorated with oranges. 2 1/2 inches high and 7 1/2 inches in diameter. Stamped faintly on base, but unreadable. Attributed to the Manatee River Pottery, Bradentown, Florida. Circa 1915-1921.

treasurer; Mary H. Ward, general manager. The directors are H.S. Glazier, E.P. Hubbell, S.A. Bean, Katherine E. McClellan, Mary H. Ward, John B. Singeltary and Mrs. B.F. Sly. (8)

Glazier, Sly, and Bean were attorneys. Glazier was elected judge and then to the state legislature. In 1923 he moved to Tampa. Sly, a Canadian, had moved to Bradentown in 1902. Hubbell was secretary of the Manatee County Board of Trade and Singeltary, a city councilman. Mary Ward had convinced the business leaders of the community to invest in her pottery.

The following year, 1918, Manatee River Pottery is listed in the St. Petersburg City Directory, and located at 21 4th N. Mrs. Ward, its manager, living at 5th Ave. N. and Bay. In February the *St. Petersburg Times* carried an article praising the Manatee River Pottery and noting, "With the single exception of Bradentown, St. Petersburg is the only city in Florida or the South which boasts of a pottery industry.... This pottery ware is fast becoming recognized as one of the true souvenirs of Florida." (9)

Persistent efforts were made to market the pottery. At the Pinellas County Fair of 1918, Mrs. Ward took first and second places in special pottery. In January of 1920, by special invitation of the Tampa Students Arts Club, Mary Ward attended the annual reception of the club at the home of Mrs. W.H. Beckwith on Bayshore Boulevard. The following story appeared in the *Tampa Morning Tribune* on January 30, 1920.

Mrs. Herrick Ward of Bradentown, who came by special invitation of the club to exhibit her beautiful pottery, was in charge of her table and very kindly showed and explained her charming display. Vases, flower bowls pitchers, and jars, in a variety of graceful shapes were shown, all made from clay from the bed of the Manatee river, and discovered by

A vase decorated with rising sun and palm trees, 6 inches high and 3 3/4 inches wide at base. Unmarked. Attributed to Manatee River Pottery, Bradentown, Florida. Circa 1915-1921 Courtesy Manatee County Historical Society.

A vase decorated with chicken egret, 3 inches wide and 4 inches high. Unmarked. Attributed to Manatee River Pottery, Bradentown, Florida. Circa 1915-1921. Courtesy: Manatee County Historical Society.

A pine tree decorated vase 6 1/4 inches high and 3 1/4 inches wide. Part of a paper label remains on the base with, "ery." Attributed to Manatee River Pottery, Bradentown, Florida. Circa 1915-1921.

Mrs. Herrick. The art has now been perfected, and Mrs. Herrick, under the name of the Manatee Pottery Co. has her own plant, and has so many orders for the ware, that she can hardly fill them. The painting, which consists principally of Florida fruit, flowers, and scenes, is done by an English decorator from the Royal Worcester Potteries. (10

The editor of the *MRJ,* commenting on manufacturing possibilities in Bradentown, gives some insight into what people thought about the pottery.

Pottery on a large scale might be made here. The fine pottery made by Mrs. Ward shows what can be done. (11)

It is difficult to know for sure exactly what happened. The *Tampa Morning Tribune* story of January 30, 1920 indicated, "Mrs. Herrick has so many orders for the ware that she can hardly fill them" and Mrs. Doud in her talk describes a busy pottery, but Mrs. Ward was not satisfied with her work in Bradentown.

Mrs. Ward had lived in New York City prior to coming to Bradentown in 1914. It is there that she likely met a young man, Henry Graack. New York is too big a city and Bradentown too far away, for Graack to have come to Bradentown by accident. In 1921 Graack traveled to Bradentown to talk about buying the Manatee River Pottery while Mrs. Ward visited with the Mayor of Orlando and the Orlando Chamber of Commerce.

In June of 1921 the front page of the *Orlando Morning Sentinel* carried the following article:

POTTERY CONCERN MAY BUILD PLANT IN ORANGE COUNTY

Kaolin Deposits Found in the County and the Making of Brick From Orange County Clay Discussed Orlando's and Orange county's future growth and

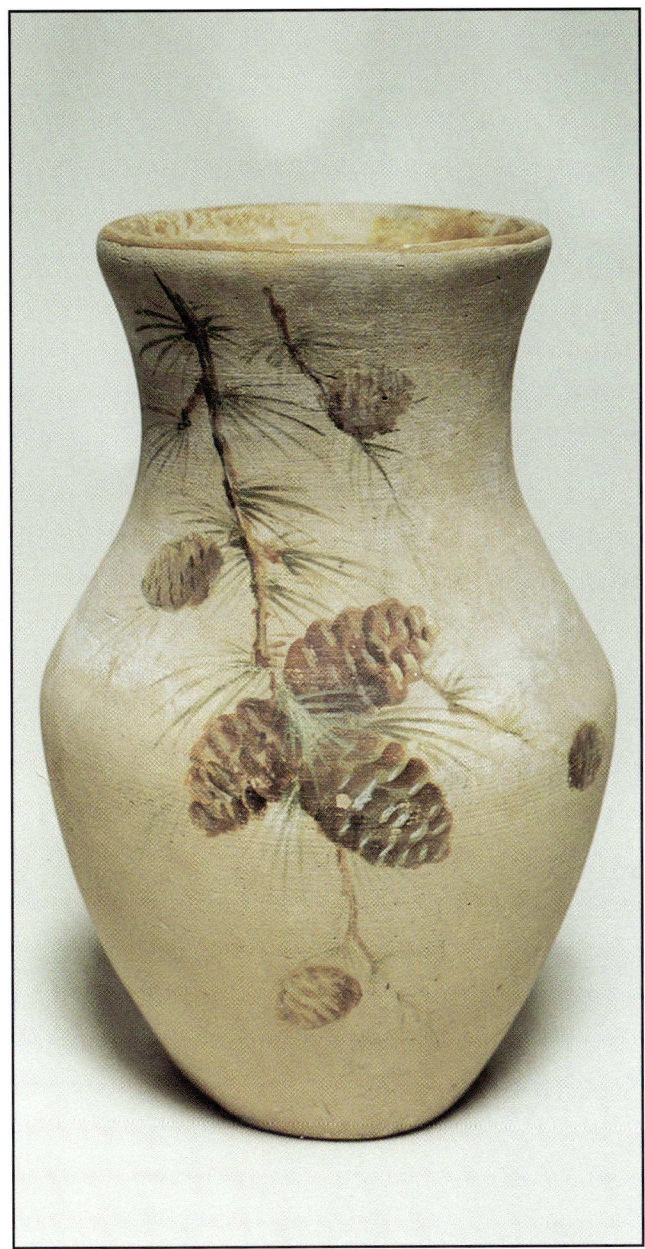

A vase with pine cones. Unmarked. Attributed to the Manatee River Pottery, Bradentown, Florida. Circa 1915-1921.

development is never lost sight of by the members of the Orlando Chamber of Commerce, and at the noon luncheon of this live business organization held yesterday... Mayor Eugene Duckworth brought samples of products made from Orlando county clay and told stories of how this clay existed like, "acres of diamonds". He had the samples to show the superiority of Orange county clay over that being produced in other sections of the state and he stated that the Manatee River Pottery Company, located at Bradentown stood ready to move their plant to Florida's Seventh City having been convinced of the great superiority of the raw material that existed in Orange county for their output.

Members of the Chamber enthusiastically endorsed the proposal of Mr. Duckworth that the invitation be extended to the Bradentown concern to cast their future with this section, and a resolution was passed to this effect. Mrs. Mary Ward, who for five years has conducted the business of the Manatee River Pottery Company, has made a substantial success of her venture. With limited capital and equipment she has turned out a finished product that has found a ready market.

In speaking of the location of this concern in Orlando, Mayor Duckworth stated that Mrs. Ward did not wish the Chamber of Commerce to offer any free site or guarantes of any kind. It was only the endorsement and recognition by this body of the soundness and possibility of such a business venture. It is understood that the plant the new concern will build here will require increased capital and possibly stock in the enterprise will be offered for sale locally. (12)

Mary Ward was planning to move her pottery to Orlando perhaps for the better clay found there but more likely because capital was more readily available. At the same time the Graacks, father and son, were planning to move to Bradentown.

A large vase decorated with a banana tree, 11 inches high and 4 1/2 inches wide. Marked on base Manatee River Pottery Inc., Bradentown, Florida. Circa 1915-1921 Courtesy Manatee County Historical Society.

IDENTIFICATION

All pottery produced at the Manatee River Pottery was unglazed on the outside and the earliest pieces coated with varnish on the inside to give some waterproofing. The first pottery produced was very coarse in texture due to the crude refining technique used by Mrs. Ward, with her children stomping about in the mud to break up the clay. When the pottery was chartered in 1917, money was available to purchase a high temperature kiln and clay refining improved, resulting in pottery with a smooth unglazed finish on the outside and a clear glaze on the inside. The pottery was skillfully and beautifully hand painted with Florida scenes. Some pottery is crudely decorated and may reflect early production. Pottery is stamped, "MANATEE RIVER POTTERY INC. BRADENTOWN, FLORIDA" Remnants of a paper label have been found on pottery that is likely Manatee River. Therefore some pottery may in the future be found with a paper label or unmarked but identified by the distinctive unglazed clay and hand painted decoration. Artist signed pieces exist.

Stamped mark found on the base of Manatee River Pottery.

Chapter Five

Henry A. Graack, Senior. The veteran potter at his wheel. Bradentown, Florida circa. 1921-1923.

The Graack Pottery
Bradenton, Florida
1921-1923

In 1913 a young potter, Henry A. Graack Jr. from Kolding, Denmark came to America to avoid the Danish draft. He worked as a valet to earn his passage on a ship that brought him to New York City. Ironically, he was drafted into the United States Army, but avoided service in Europe. Henry A. Graack Sr. joined his son sometime later. Father and son came to Florida in 1921 to take over the Manatee River Pottery. (1) The Graacks, experienced potters, were sure they could make a pottery profitable in Bradentown. It's likely that Mrs. Ward and the Graacks were friends in New York, possibly in a pottery. Mrs. Ward stayed briefly to help the Graacks and then sold her home in Bradentown and moved to Orlando where she started production of the new Orlando Potteries at the same time that the Graacks were beginning the Graack Pottery in Bradentown.

In August of 1921, just one month after a headline in the *Orlando Morning Sentinel* announced that the Manatee River Pottery Works had bought some land in Orlando, the following article appeared in the *MRJ*.

<u>NEW POTTERY</u>

The H.A. Graack and Son Art Pottery is the newest enterprise to locate in Bradentown. Mr. Graack is from Kolding, Denmark and has been in the pottery business in his native country for many years. His son has lived in New York and is familiar with the business. Mr. Graack and his son have leased the building

The home of the Graacks in Kolding, Denmark. Note the sign which reads, " H. A. GRAACK POTTEMAGER." Circa1900. Photograph courtesy Mrs. Madelyn Graack Peterson.

made to pay here said Mr. Graack. (2)

In February of 1922 the GRAACK POTTERY was exhibiting at the South Florida Fair in Tampa. The *Manatee River Journal and Bradentown Herald [MRJBH]* in a long article on the Fair, states:

Cover of GRAACK POTTERY brochure, published by the Manufacturing Jewelers Export Company. Circa 1921-1923.

A vase decorated with 2 palm trees on water with light house in background, 8 1/2 inches high and 5 inches wide. Stamped on base, THE GRAACK POTTERY, HAND MADE / HAND PAINTED, BRADENTOWN, FLA. Circa 1921-1923.

formerly occupied by Mrs. Ward's pottery and are now busy making pottery for the winter season. They expect to do a retail and wholesale business. Many new designs will be exhibited in the sales rooms and as nearly all of it will be decorated by skilled artists they will manufacture a product that will be very attractive to the curio trade. There is no reason why a good pottery can not be

Winning much admiration is the display of pottery from the Graack Pottery at Bradentown.... Recently one of the largest concerns in New York City, which had been handling Graack ware in a small way, was interested in the quality of the product and the president of the company came to Bradentown and negotiated a contract with the Graacks for the marketing of their entire output, stating that their product is among the very finest in the United States. (3)

In June the *MRJ,* as part of the July 4th celebration, the Graack Pottery announced:

A sale for the benefit of the home folks. Now is the time to secure some pretty pieces of pottery for home decoration. The sale will continue until our stock is exhausted. Come early and secure the best— at low prices.(4)

On New Year Day 1923 the *MRJBH* ran the following article.

BRADENTOWN POTTERY TO ADVERTISE TOWN Will be Shown to Realtors at Jax. Fine Exhibit Arranged for and 200 Trays to be Given away as Souvenirs Bradentown will get some very worthwhile advertising at the gathering of the National Association of Real Estate Boards, to be held at Jacksonville Jan.17-20.... Likewise one of the most important industries of this city, the Graack Pottery, will have its wares shown to "live wire" men from all parts of the country and Canada.

Thursday Secretary Wallace, while on a visit to the local association of Realtors, was taken to the Graack Pottery. He was greatly surprised at the size and character of the industry and immediately

A bud vase decorated with sun and palm tree, 5 inches high and 3 3/4 inches wide at the base. Marked on base, "The Graack Pottery, Hand Made/ Hand Painted, Bradentown, Florida." Circa 1921- 1923. Courtesy Manatee County Historical Society.

A vase with three palm trees and water. height 9 inches. Marked on base The Graack Pottery, Handmade/Hand Painted, Bradentown, Fla.

RETAIL PRICE LIST

VASES

No.	Height	Decoration	Price Decorated	Price Undecorated
2A	6	Poppies	$3.75	$2.55
2B	8½	Cranes	9.00	6.00
3B	8½	Indian Girl (moon)	9.00	6.00
3C	10	Colonial Girl	13.50	9.00
7A	6	Florida Scene	3.75	2.55
7B	7	Oriental Girl	6.00	3.90
7C	8½	Parrot	9.00	6.00
7D	10	Egyptian Girl	13.50	9.00
9	10	Love Birds	18.00	12.00
12A	7	Tulips	6.00	3.90
12B	8½	Florida Scene	9.00	6.00
12C	10	Peacock	15.00	9.00
14A	6	Iris	3.75	2.55
14B	7	Daffodils	6.00	3.90
14C	8½	Indian Girl	9.00	6.00
14D	10	Duck and Moon	13.50	9.00
15	10	Peacock	18.00	12.00
22A	6	Roses	3.75	2.55
22B	7	Butterflies	6.00	3.90
34A	8½	Flowers	9.00	6.00
34B	10	Pine Cones	13.50	9.00
68A	8½	Flowers	9.00	6.00
68B	10	Swan Scene	13.50	9.00
68C	12	Northern Boat Scene	18.00	12.00

BUD VASES

No.	Height	Decoration	Price Decorated	Price Undecorated
66A	7½	Conventional	3.45	2.25
66B	9	Bird and Blossoms	4.50	3.00

CANDLESTICKS

No.	Height	Decoration	Price Decorated	Price Undecorated
60A	5	Bird and Blossoms	2.25	1.50
60B	9	Peacock and Fountain	5.25	3.45

LAMPS

No.	Height	Decoration	Price Decorated	Price Undecorated
23	10	Conventional	25.50	16.50
24	8½	Russian Dancer	21.00	15.00
25	8½	Butterfly and Blos.	21.00	15.00

BOWLS

No.	Diameter	Decoration	Price Decorated	Price Undecorated
1A*	5	Flowers	1.95	1.20
1B	6	Pine Cones	3.30	2.10
1C	7	Pond Lilies	4.50	3.00
1D	8	Nasturtiums	6.00	3.90
1E	9	Seagulls	12.75	8.25
4A	5	Conventional	2.25	1.50
4B	6	Violets and Pansies	3.75	2.55
4C	7½	Pheasant and Blossoms	7.50	4.95
4D	8½	Oak Leaves	12.75	8.25

FRUIT URN

No.	Diameter	Decoration	Price Decorated	Price Undecorated
50	8½	Grapes	18.00	12.00

* Stem holders for this bowl, .50 and $1.00, according to size.

Special pieces furnished to order.

Price list from Graack pottery sales brochure.

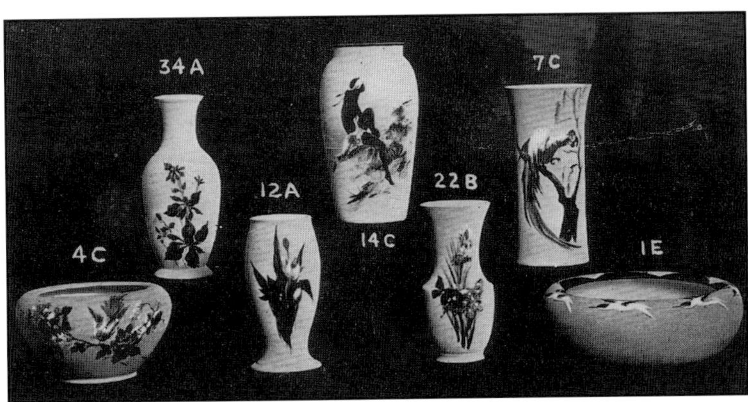

Pottery samples, catalogue numbers and price list from the the sales brochure titled, GRAACK POTTERY published by the Manufacturing Jewelers Export Company, Inc. 54 Dey Street, New York, N.Y.. Circa 1921-1923. The brochure was given to the author by Madelyn Graack Peterson.

A bowl decorated with hummingbird and roses, 4 inches high and 8 inches wide. Stamped on base, THE GRAACK POTTERY, HAND MADE/ HAND PAINTED, BRADENTOWN, FLA. Circa 1921-1923.

arranged for the shipment of 200 pintrays which he purchased for the Jacksonville Realtors Association, to be distributed among the 700 delegates which will attend the national gathering. Each of the pins will have a poinsettia painted on it.

"I had no idea such an industry as this pottery existed anywhere in Florida" said Mr. Wallace. "It is important that these people who are coming here see something of what we produce besides winter resorts and citrus fruits, palms and flowers.... I hope to have exhibits of a number of articles manufactured in this state but none of these can be more interesting than a pottery exhibit such as will come from the Graack place."

Arrangements have been made with the Messrs. Graack to send some of their larger wares for exhibit. Some fine specimens of the pottery's products are now being displayed at the Manatee County Publicity Department headquarters and attracting much favorable comment. (5)

In March of 1923 the *MRJ* contains a lengthy description of the Graack Pottery originally published in a booklet by the Manufacturing Jewelers Export Company, Inc. of New York City. It is a romantic description of Graack pottery that expresses the rhetoric of the time perfectly.

GRAACK POTTERY IS ADVERTISING CITY

Is The Subject Of Fine Booklet Sent Over Country and Abroad By New York Concern Which Buys Entire Product

Some time ago this newspaper carried a news story telling about closing of a contract between the Graack Pottery of this city and the Manufacturing Jewelers Export Company Inc. of New York City, whereby the big New York concern contracted to buy the entire

A candle stick, or bud vase, with palm trees and water. Stamped on base, THE H. A. GRAACK & SON, ART POTTERY, BRADENTOWN, FLA. Circa 1921-1923.

A candlestick, or bud vase, decorated with poinsettias, 8 inches high and 3 3/4 inches wide at the base. Marked on the base, " The H. A. Graack and Son Art Pottery, Bradentown, Florida. ca 1921-1923.

output of the local pottery and market it.

The contract was closed after the head of the New York concern had come here and personally looked into the pottery concerns product and possibilities. He stated that he has been attracted here by the quality of the ware, some of which had been sold to his concern, and his interest was so much aroused that he came here to make a personal inspection, and that trip led to the making contact to take all of the ware the Bradentown concern could turn out.

Already the Manufacturing Jewelers Export company Inc. is giving Bradentown some great advertising throughout the country and abroad. It has had a booklet printed illustrating the pottery business as carried on here. The title page carries the words "Graack Pottery" and this is above a cut of a beautiful vase, artistically decorated and printed in six colors to reproduce exactly the colors in the artists work.

The remainder of the booklet is given over to the story of "Graack Pottery— Made By Hand." as the subtitle page announces, together with a number of beautiful halftones in velvety black showing the process of making the pottery, also examples of the work. The subject matter is reproduced herewith in full:

In America appreciation of good pottery is growing rapidly. What is even more interesting, we like pottery made in America, of American clay, with a bit of the wild beauty and freshness of our own country about it—modern pottery, made by master craftsmen of this age old art. For pottery is the oldest of all crafts and the progress of all peoples who have ever lived on the earth is revealed through their pottery.

We do not need to draw heavily on our

A bowl decorated with pine cones, 4 1/2 inches high and 6 1/2 inches wide. Marked on base, " The Graack Pottery, Hand Made/ Hand Painted, Bradentown, Florida." Circa 1921-1923. Courtesy Manatee County Historical Society.

A vase decorated with an Iris, 6 inches high and 3 1/2 inches wide. Marked on bottom, "H. A. Graack and Son, Art Pottery, Bradentown, Florida." ca 1921-1923.

imagination to visualize the origin of this art. When man left the treetops his needs began to multiply. What more natural than that he should fashion from the earth a crude cup for drinking——a jug to hold his drink. These primitive vessels were hardened only by the suns rays. Then somewhere through the ages he discovered the use of fire and in a crude oven baked his pots and jugs. In the beginning pottery was fashioned by the hand alone, but into the mind of some long ago forgotten man mauling over his pots of clay, there one day came a vision—if the plastic clay could be given a circular motion while working, vessels of far greater symmetry and utility could be made. From that vision was born the potters wheel, which is used today in making pottery by hand in practically the same form as when records of it first crept into history.

Have you ever seen a potter at work? It is worth a long journey to see a master potter at his wheel. No art is quite so simple so primitive. The one and only tool necessary is a potters wheel or thrower's wheel, as it is sometimes called. This consists of a wooden disc about 12 inches in diameter joined by a connecting rod to a heavier disc. With the smaller disc at the top, this is set in a frame so that it may be revolved rapidly. Power is applied to the lower wheel, sometimes by a motor, but most potters prefer to furnish their own power by foot. A potters wheel and the bare hands of the potter—we may say that this is all, but these alone will no more create a piece of pottery than a flowing brush and a pot of paint will create a deathless canvas. Back of the potters hands there must be the artist's vision with its fitting shapes of beauty.

The potter sits at his wheel. He takes a

A vase decorated with a waterfall, 5 3/8 inches at the base and 13 1/2 inches high. Marked on base, " The H. A. Graack and Son Art Pottery, Bradentown, Florida." Circa 1921-1923. Courtesy Manatee County Historical Society.

lump of plastic clay carefully prepared to be of the right consistency and places it on the upper wheel. With a swing of his foot he starts the wheel spinning.

Softly invitingly, his deft fingers enter and feel about the revolving mass. Swiftly before our astonished vision the clay takes shape, rises, spreads out, contracts at the potters will. In a few minutes it is finished. The wheel stops. Where a moment before lay a mass of shapeless clay there now stands a bowl—a vase, of exquisite beauty. We are silenced by the skill of the artist. The wonder magic of creation has been performed before our eyes. It is more than a revelation. It is symbolic of the Master Craftsman Himself, standing behind the veil of the unknown, creating new worlds and tossing them into eternity.

Not long ago a potter walked beside the Manatee river in southern Florida. The tide was out and a wide strip of the bottom of the river could be seen. The brooding eyes of the potter dreamed down through the exposed mud and silt to the clay beneath and rare and lovely shapes rose before him—pottery of a natural tint so soft and beautiful that a touch of the glorious sunshine of Florida seemed imprisoned in its clay, pottery with a breath of the near sea about it and a bit of the exotic life and color of the tropics caught to its surfaces by an artists brush.

From that vision of the potter has come the beautiful handmade Graack Pottery of today. H. A. Graack Sr., artistic genius of the pottery which bears his name, came from Denmark and represents the third generation of his family who have devoted their lives to this art; thus the cumulative skill of three generations of artisans finds expression at his finger tips.

He is intimately familiar with all forms of this classic art and personally makes all of the more massive and artistic pieces. No single piece, be it small or large is allowed to leave the pottery until it has his approval.

It has long been known that clay deposits found in Florida are peculiarly adapted to the making of pottery. Le Moyne de Morgues writing in the sixteenth century, gives illustrations of forms used at that time. In 1761 and 1766 Josiah Wedgewood had Florida clays sent to him in England for experimentation and pronounced them good. But only in recent years have Florida clays taken there rightful place in the production of pottery. The clay used in making Graack pottery is taken from the bottom of the Manatee river below Bradentown. When the tide is out the river bottom is uncovered to a depth of eight or ten feet, at which depth the clay is found.

It is taken to the pottery where it is sifted and washed several times until all silt and impurities are removed and only the smooth, pure clay remains. More than half of the cubic content is lost in this process. It is then brought to the right consistency for the potters work. No coloring of any kind is used and the peculiar soft tint of the finished pottery is due to the clay itself.

When the potters work is done the various pieces are first dried by natural process, unaided by either artificial heat or the sun's rays. This requires about three weeks, during which time it has to be turned and inspected frequently to see that the drying is uniform. It is doubtful if any pottery, anywhere, is made with more exacting care and attention to every detail. After drying has been com-

A wall pocket decorated with orange tree branch, oranges and orange blossoms. Unmarked but attributed to Graack Pottery, Bradentown, Florida Circa 1921-1922. Courtesy of Manatee County Historical Society,

pleted it is fired in a double kiln, a steady white heat being maintained for about twenty hours.

Graack pottery as it comes from the kiln is so beautiful in color and general appearance that its exterior is left unglazed and its rich tint of delicate terra cotta or bisque harmonizes with all sorts of surroundings; indeed it is beautiful under any and all conditions. A special white glaze coats the interior and renders it impervious to the effects of water. The result is a practical and ornamental ware which can be readily cleaned. Being of hard and uniform texture throughout, when badly soiled or slightly damaged through careless handling, it may be quickly resurfaced with a piece of fine sand paper. For ordinary cleaning a dry or damp cloth is sufficient.

The one feature of Graack pottery, however, which distinguishes it from all others, is its suitability for decoration. Its natural color, harmonizing as it does with all settings, also furnishes a background for the artists brush that cannot be surpassed. This feature was recognized so early by the makers that up to the present they have not offered it undecorated, but have found a ready sale for their entire production decorated by their own artists. Increased production, however, now makes it possible to offer it without decoration. The range of decorative treatment that can be applied to Graack pottery is almost unlimited, from the simplest designs to landscapes and marine views. It takes any and all colors.

It would be futile to attempt to describe the many and beautiful decorated pieces of Graack pottery now offered by the makers. Like anything produced by the hum an hand it has to be seen to be appreciated. The illustrations printed herein and even the cover design, reproducing a Graack vase in color, give a very inadequate idea of the beauty of the pottery itself. To see it made, however, is to renew our faith in the ultimate survival of handicraft, even in this machine ridden age, and surely this pottery of our own land, with a breath of romance about it, is wholesome pottery to have in any home.

Graack Pottery is supplied to the trade only through the Manufacturing Jewelers Export Company, Inc., 54 Dey St., New York. (6)

Henry Graack, the old Danish potter, and his son must have had dreams of building a major national pottery in Bradentown, and with the signing of a contract with the Manufacturing Jewelers Export Company, it certainly looked like they were on their way to success. All that was needed was the capital to build the pottery. An article in the November 8, 1923 issue of the *MRJBH* indicates that there were problems in Bradentown.

GRAACK POTTERY TO BE ENLARGED SOON Will Establish Stores in Other Cities For the Sale of Their Fine Wares Manufactured in Bradentown. An enlarged Graack pottery at Bradentown, instead of that fine and growing manufacturing industry leaving here, as was contemplated a few weeks ago. A bit of effort on the part of a few enterprising citizens and assurances of the Graacks father and son, that the capital they need to expand their business will be forth coming—that turned the trick and the pottery, which is an industry in Florida peculiar to Bradentown, and whose wares are advertising this city far and wide, was saved for the town.

The Graacks, desiring to branch out and get a field where expansion would be easier, had gone so far as to buy a building in Jacksonville where they could manufacture and display and sell their wares. Then the matter was taken in hand by the board of trade, and members of that body finally gave the Graacks assurance that the capital necessary for expansion here would be forthcoming. That was all that was necessary.

"Now," said Mr. Graack, Jr. to a Herald man Monday, "we are just finishing unpacking the goods we had packed. We are glad to remain in Bradentown. Our business has become identified as a Bradentown business; our wares have all borne the name 'Bradentown' and we feel attached to this city. We shall expand the business from here. We hope to establish stores of our own for sale of our wares, in various Florida cities. Here we are at the source of our raw materials supply, for our wares are made entirely from Manatee county clays...."

Some day the Graack pottery will be an industry that will loom large in the business life of Bradentown.

Just now the Graacks are experimenting with some new clays they have discovered which seem to be splendid for manufacture of brick, tile and flower pots. They have made up some miniature bricks for samples. The bricks are of a warm red in color, the color being uniform and the texture fine. "That is merely an experiment," said the younger Mr. Graack, "but I anticipate that eventually we will be manufacturing flower pots in large numbers out of that clay." (7)

The November 8, 1923 article is the last trace of the Graacks in Manatee county. Apparently the capital needed to expand the Graack Pottery business as promised by the Bradentown Board of Trade was never raised. Stories in the *MRJ* in July and September of 1916 gives some insight into the problem.

At a Bradentown Board of Trade meeting in July of 1916, William Schlecht a well known citizen of Bradentown was given the floor. Mr. Schlecht, a manufacturer of a palmetto fiber brush products made a proposition to the Board in which he asked them to appoint a committee to investigate his plant, go thoroughly into the capacity and cost of production and make a thorough examination of his business in full and if the committee was satisfied that it was a sound investment and a good thing for Bradentown, he would ask a certain amount of financial backing. (8)

On the evening of Monday Sept. 18, 1916, at a meeting of the Board of Trade, the Bradentown Brush Company was organized with a capital stock of $15,000. (9) Mr. Schlecht got the money to expand his business, and the next year Mrs. Mary Ward, in a process that was probably similar to Schlecht's, raised $10,000 to start her pottery. The Graacks were not long time Bradentown residents and they were probably not experienced businessmen. It is also likely that the Board of Trade was aware of marketing problems that the Orlando Potteries were experiencing. In any event the issue must have been warmly debated by the Board before their request was finally turned down. Undoubtedly a disappointment for the Graacks.

The Graacks left Bradentown in 1924, Henry Sr. for his home in Kolding, Denmark and Graack Jr. back to New York City. The younger Graack was not finished in his attempts to be a successful potter in Florida and 11 years later he would return to Ocala and the Silver Spring.

IDENTIFICATION

Pottery produced by Henry H. Graack and son is similar in appearance to Manatee River Pottery but the unglazed exterior finish, a light brown in color, is finer and smoother. The interior is glazed a cream color. The pottery is stamped, THE GRAACK POTTERY, HAND MADE, HAND PAINTED, BRADENTOWN, FLA. or THE H. A. GRAACK & SON ART POTTERY, BRADENTOWN, FLA.

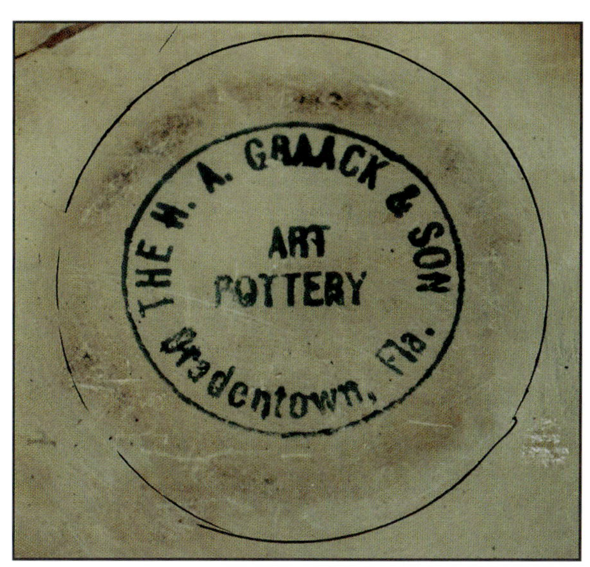

Stamped marks found on the base of Graack Pottery.

Chapter Six

Mary Ward, with sun bonnet, sits with Henry Graack, Sr., front left, Miss Denise Shields, front right. Others unknown. This photograph was probably taken in the summer of 1921. The Graacks had arrived in Bradentown and Mrs. Ward was leaving for the Orlando Potteries.

Orlando Potteries
1921-1926

Mary Ward sold her home in Bradentown and in the summer of 1921 moved to Orlando. Settling in at the Peppercorn Apartments on East Church Street, a street then canopied with large Florida oaks, Mary began the work of building a pottery to be located on the old Apopka road in Fairvilla near the present day Orange County Country Club.

In July of 1921 the *Orlando Morning Sentinel* carried the following:

NEW INDUSTRY FOR ORLANDO Pottery Company Buys Tract of Land Near City, Is Erecting Building. Orlando is destined to become a great artistic center. The Manatee River Pottery Works, Inc. has bought a tract of land on the main line of the Dixie Highway just outside the city limits and has already begun the construction of the first wing of its factory. The hustling firm of Wallace & Bailey Realtors, is responsible for the initial steps in attracting this new industry to the advantages of abundant raw materials, a large market, and exceptional location offered by Orlando. No fewer than thirty people will be employed and these will be highly skilled workmen for the most part.

The artistic instinct of the race has reached some of the highest achievements in the form of pottery. Exquisitely wrought vases have inspired some of the most beautiful poetry in our language. By many critics, Keats' Ode to a Grecian Urn is called the finest short poem in all literature. In a small way the Manatee River Pottery Works, Inc., has been producing some of the finest pottery in America. As souvenirs of Florida scenes the industry

A vase 3 3/4 inches high and 3 inches wide decorated with Florida lake scene. Marked on back of vase, " Souvenir Subtropical Midwinter Festival, Orlando, Florida." Attributed to Orlando Potteries, Orlando, Florida. Circa 1921-1926.

has already rendered incalculable service in advertising abroad the natural beauty of the state....(1)

In September the Orlando and Bradentown Chambers of Commerce met in Orlando for an enthusiastic get together. Judge Glazier of Bradentown, the president of the Manatee River Pottery was present and clearly must have known and agreed to the pottery's relocation. (2)

Later that month, on September 30, the *OMS* carried the following story:

IDOLS OF CLAY-LYRIC POEM FROM CLAY OF OLD ORANGE "Dream Spinners," With Potter's Wheel and Artist's Brush, Busy Factory on Apopka Road Near Orlando. Shortly the name Orlando, stamped into the products

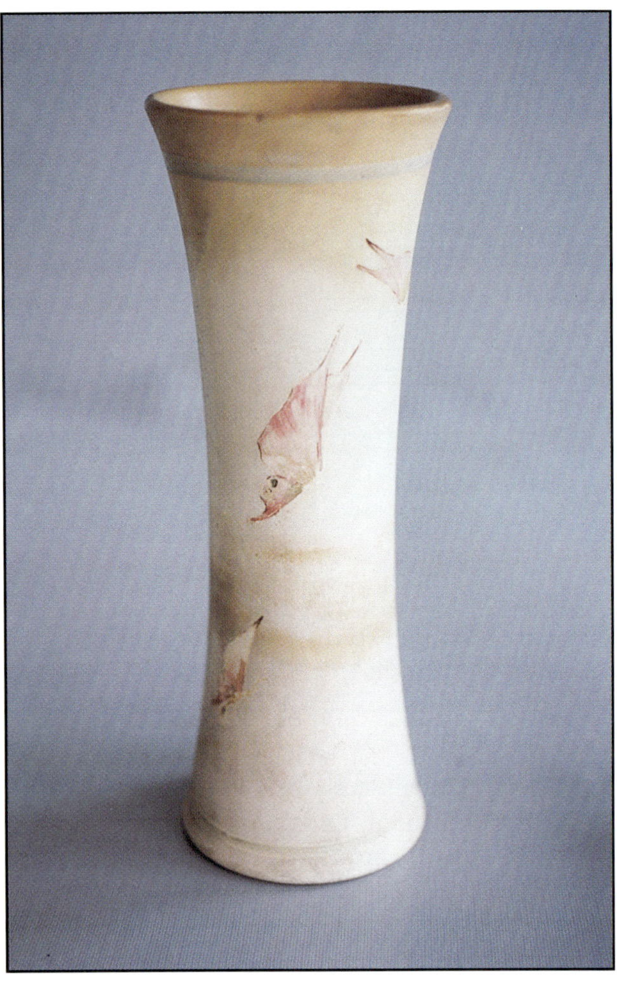

An Orlando Potteries vase with three butterflies. The top and base decorated with typical circumferential decorative lines. The base stamped faintly, ORLANDO POTTERIES FLORIDA and signed, "Vanderpool." Height 8 1/2 inches, base and mouth 3 inches. Orlando Potteries, Orlando, Florida. Circa 1921-1926.

of the Orlando Potteries will be borne on the wings of commerce throughout the United States, if the vision of eight Orlando business men and an auburn haired woman is realized. With the clay of old Orange the potter's wheel and the artist's brush, like dream spinners, are busy on the Apopka road about three miles from the City Beautiful. On August 19th last, from the potter's wheel, G. D. Krebs, secretary and treasurer of the new concern, took the first delicate vessel of clay. Yesterday he proudly displayed to the Sentinel this first product, a crude reminder, when compared with the beautiful pottery since turned out, of the magical progress made in a little over a month's operation....

Saturday morning at the Yowell-Drew fall opening, the citizens of Orlando will have the opportunity of admiring, as we have done, the beautiful products of the Orlando Potteries. It will be the first placing of the products of the new concern on the market. But a little trip out on the Apopka road, where the "dream spinners" are at work, and you come back, as we did, in a poetic vein.

A pile of clay. It came from the pits of old Orange. Mr. Krebs and Mr. Wilson, directors of the new company, stated that they had it in abundance within easy hauling distance. Three careful washings and the sand is removed. The "baker" kneads it to the point where it is ready to go on the potter's wheel. Beneath the skilled hands of the potter... it rises into a magical urn. After being dried sufficiently the vessels are placed in the baking oven. One is built to hold a thousand; another in the course of construction will have a capacity of between six and eight hundred.

Eighteen hours intervene, with carefully regulated heat, before the pottery is ready for the polishing and smoothing wheel. Then it goes to be finished and its beauty enhanced by the artist's brush. A white enameled finish on the interior makes it water proof and smooth. Where it rests on the surface of mahogany a magical coat, a secret of the Orlando Potteries is given it, insuring not the slightest scratch.

The officers and directors of the Orlando Potteries are as follows: M. J. Daetwyler, president; Mrs. M. H. Ward, vice president and manager; G. D. Krebs, secretary treasurer. The directors: M. J. Daetwyler, G. D. Krebs, N. P. Yowell, H. S. Wilson, Mrs. M. H. Ward, F. O. King, John A. McCullough, S. Kendrick Guernsey, Allison Palmer. (3)

The first advertisement for Orlando Potteries appeared in the *Sentinel* on December 8, 1921 in the Yowell-Drew Christmas display ad and reads:

Beautiful Orlando Pottery sold in this city exclusively by this store. This product made in Orlando is without a doubt an artist's ambition fully realized. It is made up in many styles of vases and decorated with loveliness of Florida's scenery.

In March of 1922 the pottery was purchased by N. P. Yowell and his associates. Yowell was the president of the Chamber of Commerce and one of two principal owners of Yowell-Drew, the largest department store in Orlando. Yowell enlarged the pottery, ordered new machinery and began manufacture of the pottery on a large scale. Plans were made to sell Orlando Pottery, "in all parts of the country." (4)

Yowell-Drew ran a full page ad in the *OMS* on May 9th under the title, "Yowell Drew Company

A miniature bowl 1 1/2 inches high and three inches wide decorated with blue pansies and a broad circular blue band. Stamped on base, " ORLANDO POTTERIES, FLORIDA." Circa 1921-1926.

Two candlesticks made at the Orlando Potteries. One tilted on its side reveals a paper label and a hole in the base indicating that the piece may have been made in a mold. Courtesy of Doug White, Orlando, Florida.

Store News" and Mary Ward wrote a brief history of the Orlando Potteries in which she noted:

Orlando Potteries is the history of the development of the clay industry of the state. The clay is found in old abandoned pits that for years past have furnished material for some of the finest roads in Florida.

Potters and clay experts from all over the country have pronounced these deposits of unusual value, for the clay after being fired is of such remarkable texture and color that it has the appearance of having a dull transparent glaze in color ranging from a light terra cotta to a delicate ivory.

The ware takes a hard fire without the addition of any foreign clays and because of its subtle beauty, strength and uniqueness the demand for it has far exceeded the capacity of the present plant, and the potters at their wheels are working overtime making objects of art and beauty from clay that for so long was unknown save to the Seminole Indians more than a century ago.

In making this pottery the inside only is glazed, leaving the outside as it comes from the kiln, like so many of the old

A group of candlesticks with speckled Yale blue glaze. Small candlesticks height 5 inches base 4 inches in diameter. Medium candlestick height 8 inches base 4 inches in diameter. Tall candlesticks height 12 1/4 inches base 4 3/4 inches in diameter. Each bearing a paper label on base, " ORLANDO POTTERIES, FLORIDA." Circa 1921-1926.

A bowl decorated with pine cones and a circular band below and around neck of bowl. 4 inches high and 6 1/2 inches wide. Base has characteristic indentation and circular turning marks. Base marked in pencil, "#7-S". Attributed to Orlando Potteries, Orlando, Florida. Circa 1921-1926.

Egyptian and Grecian pieces. The surface is so hard when fired that it does not soil easily, and can be readily cleaned with a dry or a damp cloth. The jar should not be embedded in water, because of the unequal expansion of the clay and the glaze when saturated." (5)

In August of 1922 the *Orlando Morning Sentinel* carried an exciting article about the pottery.

ORLANDO POTTERIES IS FAST BECOMING A LARGE INDUSTRY Twenty Persons Are Now Employed In Turning Out Products Of Local Company. Orders Booked Ahead. The Orlando Potteries is expanding in all directions and bids fair to become one of the largest industries in central of south Florida in years to come. The group of buildings, including those used for kilning, workrooms, artist's studio, store rooms, etc., are daily putting out exquisitely formed and painted pottery by the scores, and as soon as they are finished are shipped immediately to the North, West and East and throughout the South.

Twenty persons are now employed in the making of the beautiful pottery, each piece of which helps to advertise The City Beautiful in northern markets. There are now six artists and several more have been engaged from Chicago art schools. According to Chas. Rybolt, secretary and treasurer of the corporation, artists are difficult to procure but he hopes to have at least fourteen for the coming season. Samples are carried at Yowell-Drew Co., and this is the only retail place of Orlando potteries in the South. More than 1,700 pieces were sold by this concern in the month of December. Mr. Rybolt stated, and next season will undoubtedly see a record business with the pottery. The company has more than $5,000 of orders ahead.

Some of the most attractive vases, bowls and jars are of Florida scenery. Stately palms bordering a lake at the setting of the sun, a lake filled with pond lilies in bloom, or sprays of white orange blossoms are among the attractive designs that speak of the tropical beauties of Florida. The texture of the pottery is a special feature, the finish being of a velvety quality. (6)

Two weeks before Christmas of 1922 the *OMS* informed its readers,

ORLANDO POTTERIES TO OPEN SALESROOM AT ITS PLANT SOON. Nation Wide Sales Plan Will Be Developed Opening Of Display Quarters On Apopka Road This Week. The Orlando Potteries, a subsidiary of the Yowell-Drew Company, will open its new sales room on the Apopka road, three miles outside Orlando on Thursday or Friday of this week, it was announced yesterday.

The building is just being completed and will be used for sales and display purposes in connection with the plan to introduce the products of Orange county's clay all over the United States.

W. B. Stephenson will have charge of the sales force and expects to have the pottery on display in all of the larger cities in the country within the next six months. It will be a splendid advertisement for Orlando and Orange county, Mr. Stephenson believes. The Orlando Potteries Company was established considerably more than a year ago and was purchased by the Yowell-Drew Company last winter. Since that time the product of the Apopka road plant has been sold in many Northern cities, but no nation-wide sales plan has been followed heretofore. (7)

A vase decorated with palm trees, clouds and a circular band above and around base. 5 1/4 inches high and 3 inches wide. Base with characteristic indentation and circular turning marks. Base marked in pencil, "#34-S." Attributed to Orlando Potteries, Orlando, Florida. Circa 1921-1926.

A week later the *Sentinel* announced on its front page:

POTTERIES COMPANY SALES ROOM READY EARLY NEXT MONTH Announcement of the opening of the new sales room of the Orlando potteries will be made within the next few days, according to Mrs. Herrick Ward, a director of the company, and actively interested in its management. The building, which adjoins the company's plant, is practically completed now.

Mrs. Ward said that arrangements has been made to sell the pottery all over America with W. R. Stephenson having charge of the sales force. The company is not, as was formerly announced, a subsidiary of the Yowell-Drew Company, though N.P. Yowell is its president. The company's stockholders, besides Mr. Yowell and Mrs. Ward, include Harry B. Wilson, Dr. C. D. Christ, G. D. Krebs, S. Kendrick Guernsey, and J. H. McCullough. (8)

Newton P. Yowell, the president of the Orlando Potteries, was born in Virginia in 1871. His family came to Orlando in 1884 and by the age of eight Yowell was working as a clerk in local dry goods stores. In 1894 Yowell opened a store of his own and then acquired five stores in other Florida cities. In 1913 Yowell formed a stock company known as Yowell-Duckworth, purchased a large lot on the corner of Orange and Central Ave. and erected the first large building in Orlando. In 1919 Mr. Yowell bought out Mr. Duckworth's interest in the business and the name was changed to Yowell-Drew Company. Yowell-Drew was a large general department store and the fourth or fifth largest business in Florida when Mr. Yowell decided to invest in the Orlando Potteries. (9)

The pottery was from its beginning a large enterprise. The Orlando City Directory for 1923 lists 14 employees including:

1. Mrs. Ella Amerman, Glazer. Orlando Pottery, Fairvilla.

2. Andrew DeVries, artist. Orlando Pottery, Fairvilla.

3. Miss Rose Gardner, artist, Orlando Pottery.

4. K. F. Green, packer, Orlando Pottery.

5. Mrs. Mabelle Green, bander, Orlando Pottery.

6. R. L. Launstein, turner, Orlando Pottery, Fairvilla.

7. John McCulloch, vice president, operations. Orlando Pottery. Home 530 E. Washington.

8. Joseph P. Nash, artist, Orlando Pottery, Fairvilla.

9. E. P. Reese, caster, Orlando Pottery.

A vase decorated with a oranges and orange branch. 5 3/4 inches high and 3 1/4 inches wide. Paper label on base, "ORLANDO POTTERIES, FLORIDA." Circa 1921-1926.

The *Orlando Magazine* published by the Orlando Chamber of Commerce for January, 1923 contains the following article.

THE ORLANDO POTTERIES
Quite in keeping with the spirit of progress and development of the City

A vase decorated with two palms growing under a purple sky, the scene covering the front and back. A typical yellow band encircles the base. The base with characteristic turnings and penciled price. Height 8 1/4 inches, mouth 5 1/4 inches and base 3 3/8 inches. Unmarked but attributed to the Orlando Potteries, Orlando, Florida. Circa 1921-1926. Courtesy of the Manatee County Historical Society.

10. W. E. Rose, pressman, Orlando Pottery, Fairvilla.

11. Ella Rose, employee, Orlando Pottery, home near North Fern Creek Avenue.

12. W. B. Stephenson, sales manager, Orlando Pottery. Home 411 E. Pine.

13. Thomas Tompkinson, potter, Orlando Pottery. Home 620 N. Garland.

14. Mrs. Mary H. Ward, general manager, Orlando Pottery, home Peppercorn Apartments.

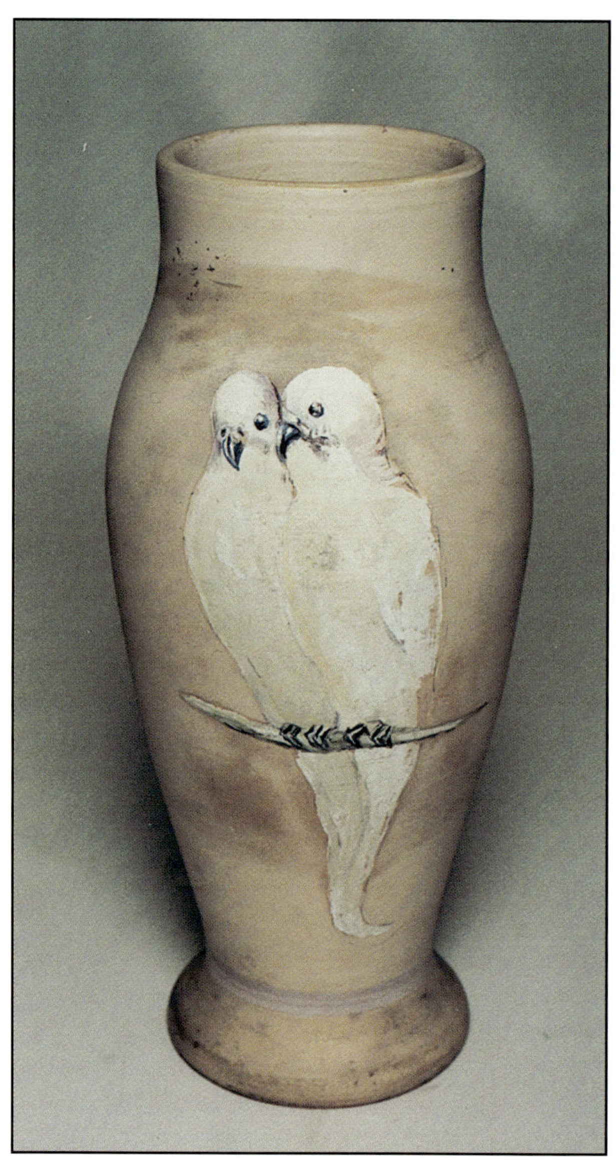

A vase decorated with love birds, 10 inches high and 4 3/4 inches wide. Marked on base, " Orlando Potteries, Orlando, Florida." Circa 1921-1926.

Beautiful are the Orlando Potteries, a local industry that is not only rapidly developing into one of the most substantial enterprises of Central Florida, but constitutes a feature in the city's commercial activities, and a most interesting and educational showplace for visitors as well as home folks.

An Orlando Potteries bud vase with palm tree decoration. Marked on the base with an ink stamp, "Orlando Potteries Florida." Courtesy, Doug White, Orlando, Florida.

An Orlando Potteries lamp base with flower decoration about base and a hole in rear for electrical wiring. Stamped on base Orlando Potteries, Florida. Height 10 1/4 inches.

The potteries are located less than three miles from Orlando on the Apopka road, having a capacity of 1800 pieces a week, the process of manufacture being most interesting to observe and to which the public has been invited by the management....

Orlando has one more claim to fame by the product of artistic clayware, and its value is being appreciated by the discriminating art buyers all over the

A green glazed bowl and two candlesticks. Orlando Potteries, Orlando, Florida. Circa 1921-1926. Courtesy: Orange County Historical Society.

country.

The clay from which the pottery is made is of wonderful fineness, and after being put in solution and through the various processes of sifting, finally through a screen of one hundred and twenty meshes to the inch which removes all sand, then through presses which squeeze all the water out, one hardly recognizes it as the same clay seen in abundance right here in Orlando. There is probably none finer for pottery anywhere in the whole country, and after it has gone through the kiln it takes on a most delicate tint, not pink, but suggesting pink, and a texture as fine as an egg shell, but with a very durable firmness.... Mr. Bartett, the chief wheelman, who learned his work in England, has been a potter for over fifty years, and shows in every motion his love for and understanding of the plastic medium which reflects his art.

Most of the heads of departments are from the old country, Mr. Reese from one of the biggest potteries in East Liverpool, Mr. Tompkinson is an English potter and Mr. George Green, the kiln man, is from East Liverpool.

There are twenty five people now employed and it is almost all hand work.

The Orlando Potteries are now putting out between two and three hundred designs and shapes, and they are finding ready market all over the country. The kiln now in use has capacity for 1800 pieces.

Mr. Hunt who comes to the potteries from Rookwood, Ohio is one of the best designers in America, and he will be quite an addition to the production end of the business. It was Mr. Hunt who designed the two beautiful jars made for Queen Elizabeth of Belgium, who was looking over the Rookwood potteries during her visit to this country and she wrote her name on each piece....

The designing and decorating room is to many persons the most interesting place in the potteries, and to Mr. Joseph Nash, a graduate of the Art Institute of Chicago, is due much of the credit for the unusually harmonious designs which characterize the new Orlando Pottery. Many of the pieces have the Florida flowers—poinsettias, predominating, with their gorgeous coloring: some have pine cones, their dull greens and browns blending perfectly with the wonderful natural tint of the clay; there are American Indian designs, suggestive of Rodin, one of a red man on a horse, with a great deal of action; some carry the atmosphere of the desert, with camels, and the spirit of the east; then there are Greek designs, beautiful classical things; geometric figures; a lofty pine, a palmetto, here a jar with a band of dull blue, there wild roses, another a band of warm brown, toning wonderfully with the natural color; bird of paradise, a flamingo, and there are some very large jars which seem to belong in an artist's studio....

There are small pieces, candlesticks, single flower vases, bowls of every shape that is good, jars and pitchers of many designs and sizes shallow pieces for low table decoration, and large vases which in design and decorative treatment would be most creditable museum pieces.

The Orlando pottery is glazed only on the inside and therefore is in particular demand for amateurs who enjoy decorating the pieces themselves. A particular advantage is that it does not require burning, as most pottery does, after it is painted.

The Yowell-Drew Company of Orlando has set aside a special department under the direction of Mrs. D. W. Elder, where a beautiful line of decorated and plain ware is being shown, and plans for the year 1923 include a national showing and distribution of the product.

During the week before Christmas, one day shipments were made to sixteen different states....

The company is composed of Orlando citizens.... The organization of artists and potters is second to none in the country, its personnel including Joseph P. Nash, Andrew De Vries and Panos Booziotes, all graduates of the Art Institute of Chicago; Mr. T. Riggs, of the Art Students League of New York; Miss Rose Gardner of Johnston, Georgia; Miss Helen M. Fuller, and Mrs. Walker, both of Orlando.

Mr. Hunt arrived in Orlando in the winter months of 1923. Hunt, from the Rookwood Pottery in Ohio was recognized as the foremost manufacturing potter in America and was now in full charge of the manufacturing department. An important development under his direction was pottery with a hard fired glaze both inside and out, in black, blue, yellow, gray and several other colors.

Twenty people were now regularly employed by the pottery and nearly five thousand pieces of the pottery were being turned out each month. Between three and four hundred dollars worth was sold at retail in Orlando and Fairvilla. (10)

The Yowell-Drew Company ran weekly full page advertising in the *Orlando Morning Sentinel* and from the December 8, 1921 issue through to the December 20, 1924 issue these ads prominently featured Orlando Pottery. The ads give some idea of the variety of pottery made including vases, candlesticks, smoking sets, tooth pick and match holders, nut bowls, flower and trinket bowls, wall vases, lamp bases and book ends. Some pottery was glazed only on the inside and the outside decorated with Egyptian, Roman and Florida scenes. Other pottery was completely glazed in bright colors of black, blue, gray, lavender and rose. Pottery was priced from 85 cents to $6.00 for plain pottery and 50 cents to $25.00 for decorated.

Mary Ward remained at the pottery until sometime after May of 1923 but probably in a role subordinate to Hunt. In May of 1923 Mary and her son, Jimmy, were visiting relatives in New York City. (11)

In November of 1923 an exhibit of the Orlando Pottery was on display in the museum at Rollins College in Winter Park and just before Christmas the pottery ran a series of daily ads in the *Sentinel* announcing a "Special Sale of Pottery at the factory. Just for a short time we are closing out our odds and ends, discontinued patterns and shapes, numbers we do not care to ship at greatly reduced prices. Beautiful for Christmas presents, on sale at the Pottery out on the Apopka road." (12) (13)

According to the newspaper reports of 1923, the pottery was producing thousands of pieces of pottery a month and had excellent local retail sales, but sometime in late 1923 or early 1924 sales must have fallen dramatically. Yowell-Drew continued to run advertisements for Orlando Pottery along with their regular ads through the spring of 1924 and in the fall of 1924, General Manager S. L. Parker had plans for beautifying the road in front of the pottery. (14) The building was improving in appearance but a sharp drop in sales can be the only explanation for the fact that sometime in 1924, nearly all those listed in the 1923 city directory, including Mary Ward, had left town.

The pottery remained in business, clearly with many less employees, and expanded its products to include faience tile.(15) Orlando Potteries had a large booth at The Orlando Fall Exhibits of 1924, a large and well publicized exhibit of products manufactured in Orlando. The *OMS* ran a front page headline on October 10, 1924, FALL EXHIBIT GREAT SUCCESS - FINE POTTERY SHOW CENTER OF INTEREST. The headline indicates that the Orlando Potteries was still, in 1924 , considered an important asset to the people of Orlando.

In February of 1925 Joseph Cheney, a prominent local citizen, bought an interest in the pottery and the *OMS* ran the following notice:

> JOE CHENEY BUYS INTEREST IN ORLANDO POTTERIES Joe Y. Chaney has purchased an interest in the Orlando Potteries and will take over the business management at once. N. P. Yowell will continue as president of the corporation. John McCullough, vice president, and Mr. Cheney, the new member of the firm, secretary and treasurer." (16)

In the Spring of 1925 Cheney ran frequent advertisements in the *Sentinel* announcing special sales of decorated and glazed lamp bases and inviting tourists to, "come out and see how pottery is made." (17) In April there was a 20% discount on decorated ware. The last *OMS* advertisement for Orlando Pottery to be included with the Yowel Drew layout ad was on April 18, 1925. The last *OMS* ad for Orlando Potteries appeared on February 24, 1926.

Mary Ward's and N. P. Yowell's dream of a successful pottery in Orlando was not fully realized. Mary worked at the pottery from its inception in 1921 through 1923. She was smart and tough enough to convince the City Fathers of Bradentown and Orlando to invest what today would be the equivalent of a million dollars in her dream of a Florida pottery. Mary Ward was one of the first female entrepreneurs in Florida. She was singularly responsible for the production of a beautiful Florida pottery that today is, like her, nearly lost to history.

Cheney Art Tile
1927-1931

In 1925 Mr. Yowell approached Joe Cheney with the idea of taking over management of the pottery. Cheney bought a part interest in Orlando Potteries and thinking that profits could be made in the tile business, sometime in 1926 purchased the remaining stock in the Orlando Potteries. In the "boom" times of 1926 a new factory was built capable of large scale tile production and in 1927 the CHENEY ART TILE Company was born.

The *OMS* of February 12, 1927 carried the following:

> CHENEY ART TILE COMPANY TO BE IN FAIR EXHIBTS HAS GOOD FUTURE. There is no one industry in Florida that has a brighter future in store for it than The Cheney Art Tile Co. of Orlando. The use of tiling has been very prevalent in all Spanish and Moorish countries for centuries and it was this civilization that introduced tiling into general practical use over the world. While in the past centuries all the work was done by hand and very artistic yet today we are able to produce art by machinery as well as to furnish the hand

product which makes the success of this institution assured. The close proximity of this factory to Spanish America will assure it of a large export business with the rapid development of Central and South America. Its central location in Florida where building and development is only in the beginning stages alone assure it of a continuous operation as it will be more than able to compete with all northern plants on account of the freight rates.

Industrial Florida says: "The Tile made in the new plant is of the finest quality and is made by two distinct processes. In one process, the various clays used are ground up and mixed in a plastic state and pressed out by hand in molds. This method produces a very rich looking tile and is the true faience product. In the other process, the clays are taken in the dry state and after being thoroughly mixed and ground to a fine powder, the tile is pressed out by a power driven machine press. This produces a more regular and more sharply defined tile and is the one most in demand. Both classes of tile are next placed in kilns and fired,

after which the glaze is applied and the firing is repeated, the temperature in both the "bisque" and glost firing being raised to 2260 degrees F.

The Faience Tile are used for bathrooms, sun parlors, mantels, store fronts and other places where beauty and permanence are desired.

The Cheney Art Tile have been endorsed by builders, architects and the people generally over the state and it is well, in building, to demand their products as they will be more reasonable, better and you will be boosting a local industry.

In this review we are glad to compliment Mr. J. Y. Cheney, the president and manager, as a man of vision who saw the opportunity to establish an industry of value and who has surmounted all obstacles and has in operation one of the leading art tile institutions in the country. (18)

In 1927 Cheney Art Tile supplied tile for millionaire homes in Palm Beach and Miami. By 1929 the tile business was profitable; Cheney Art Tile had orders for $50,000 in tile for south Florida homes. Then the Wall Street "bust" of 1929 and all orders were canceled. (19)

Cheney persisted and developed a new tile called "Valencia." Made in diamond, octagonal and hexagonal shapes, Valencia was available in red unglazed and white glazed colors. A carload of this tile went to the Women's Club of Buffalo, New York and the red tile was installed in a new building at Rollins College.

By 1931 Orlando was in the throes of the Depression. Business dropped to almost nothing. Then, one night in late August, lightning hit the factory burning it to the ground. Orlando was left with ashes, scattered art pottery and a few tile to document an interesting time in its history. (20) (21)

A small lidded Orlando Potteries box, 8 inches in diameter. Marked on base with an ink stamp, "Orlando Potteries Florida." Courtesy, Doug White, Orlando, Florida.

IDENTIFICATION

Orlando pottery was made with both glazed and unglazed outer surfaces. The earliest pottery was, like Manatee River and Graack pottery, unglazed on the outside with a bisque or matte finish. The Orlando Potteries used a fine mesh screening process in the preparation of their clay and therefore Orlando pottery has a fine, smooth, silk-like outer surface. The unglazed clay is white, ivory, light brown or terra cotta in color. Decorations included Florida scenes, flowers, birds and Egyptian and Grecian scenes. Many of the hand painted scenes have a characteristic line painted about the circumference of the vase. Many shapes and sizes were produced, from tall vases for long stemmed roses to candlesticks, lamp bases, vases, smoking sets, nut bowls, wall pockets, toothpick and match holders. In 1923 the pottery began making glazed pottery in blue, green, black yellow, and gray. Interior surfaces are covered with a clear, white or colored glaze. Pottery is marked with a paper label or ink stamped, ORLANDO POTTERIES, FLORIDA. Some unmarked examples may have a circular indentation on the base with multiple concentric circular lines from turning. Prices are often penciled on the base. Artist signed pieces exist.

The Orlando Potteries ink stamp mark.

Orlando Potteries paper label.

Base of small Orlando Potteries vase, with characteristic base turnings found on some pottery.

Chapter Seven

Addison Mizner (1872-1920). Circa 1920. Courtesy Historical Society of Palm Beach, Florida.

Los Manos Pottery
West Palm Beach, Florida
1918-1933

Addison Mizner's chronically bad leg and his friendship with Paris Singer, heir to the sewing machine fortune, led to the two men visiting Singer's Palm Beach cottage in 1918 for some sun and rest. Mizner, then an unknown but talented and flamboyant architect, would eventually become one of the recognized geniuses of American architecture and a Florida legend.(1)

Singer had purchased large tracts of land in Palm Beach and in 1918 commissioned Mizner to build a Spanish style hospital in Palm Beach for shell shocked veterans of World War I. To build a hospital or a mansion in Florida in 1918 was not an easy task. Materials had to be brought in from hundreds to thousands of miles away over Henry Flagler's relatively new railroad, resulting in months of delay and huge increases in cost.

Alex Waugh, a friend of Mizner's, was in charge of antiques and furniture reproduction for Mizner. He remembered:

> Nothing was available, no tile, a shortage of the right timber, no hardware, cement like unto gold dust, paint hard to come by, rolled steel joists a dream, and little trained labor but all these things had to be found—and now. Thus it was that... Addison set up workshops in West Palm Beach and they went far to meeting the problem, though few people realize the immense complications and difficulties Addison faced in getting the various plants into operation. Take the example of roof tile alone. These were required by the hundred squares at a time if the houses he was building were to be roofed at all, but they had to be the rounded

Spanish tile, and they were not to be had for love or money. So they had to be made and made locally and in sufficient quantities to meet the demand and right there the first snag arose. Where to find the right clay? And how to transport it over the then rough trails to a main road, itself a cart track compared to what we see today in Florida. And having done that, who knew how to construct a kiln and fire it? With what did one line the interior of the kiln? And how about firing temperatures? All these problems and they were both acute and serious in implication had to be solved, and Addison the one to solve them. Again take the lovely glazed floor tile in the Mizner blue variety for which he became famous. Thousands were wanted but how about the right pigments to stand up to kiln heat

The Los Manos Pottery with tile visible under the shed and a large kiln on the left. Courtesy Historical Society of Palm Beach County.

and what about color blending for the various shades of tile to be made…all these problems had to be worked out and by very untrained labor. (2)

The solution of these problems by Addison Mizner led to the building of the Paris Singer Pottery which would later become Los Manos Pottery, the first division of Mizner Industries.

Singer's concept of a convalescent hospital for soldiers was soon dropped as the war ended, but plans continued for a social club for wealthy winter visitors to be called The Everglades Club. Roof tile for the club was made at the pottery. White and brown Georgia clay was brought in and according to Alex Waugh:

Georgia crude kilns were constructed and fired with logs of pine, near the railroad tracks in West Palm Beach and the factory for roof tile, floor tile and other glazed clay products flourished busily. The first of its output were the roof tiles for The Everglades Club in 1919. (2)

With the completion of The Everglades Club, Mizner got a number of commissions to build winter homes for other Palm Beach residents including the Stotesbury's, the Vanderbilts and the Wannamakers. Mizner ended his relationship with Paris Singer, borrowed money from a bank, bought the pottery from Singer and established Los Manos Pottery in 1919 as a continuing source of roof and floor tile and decorative garden pottery, all in the Spanish style.

Alice DeLarna, in a letter found in the archives

A yellow and green glazed bowl. Height 7 3/8 inches, width 13 1/8 inches. Stamped on base, " Los Manos Pottery, Palm Beach, Florida." Circa 1918-1933. Courtesy Boca Raton Historical Society.

of *HSPB* regarding the Los Manos Pottery states:

In the first year Wilson Mizner (Addison's younger brother) was supposed to be in charge but Wilson was incapable of running anything. When Horace (Chase), Addison's nephew, was put in charge he was only twenty-two (bless his heart), and he was quite incapable of running anything either! From the beginning hundreds of neat wooden molds were used, set up in the yard on long trestle tables. Obviously they all had to be exactly the same size in order to fit together. The tile yard was as close as you could get to the railroad tracks and freight cars of clay were brought in from Georgia. The negroes that made the tile kneaded and beat the lumps of clay like bread dough to get all air pockets out of the clay. Then it was spread in a uniform thickness on each of the molds. It soon hardened in the sun and then they were stacked in the crude beehive shaped baking oven, made of brick. Florida pine from nearby flats were burned and after baking came out fairly uneven and gave the tiles their interesting color and texture. Go up to the top floor of the old Mizner apartment (in The Everglades Club), and look out the windows and you can see from five flights up all the roofs of Via Mizner and Via Parizi. That is the way to appreciate texture and color, variations of tile roofs. The same was true for the floor tiles. They made them the same way, beaten and kneaded clay dough on long trestle tables and they were fired in that crude kiln. They cooked unevenly, which was not good, I used to say a tile

Mizner tile

setter 'always tapped each tile with the trowel and if the sound it makes is ping then it's O.K., but if the sound is pong they discard it because it is too soft and it will erode.

A good sensible professional foreman was finally put in charge of the factory and after a few months the output was enormous. It had to be, in those early twenties an awful lot of houses were built by the Mizner organization. (3)

The *Palm Beach Weekly News* contains the following:

With characteristic initiative Mr. Mizner established the Singer hand made potteries (in 1918 the Singer Pottery, bought by Mizner in 1919), the only hand made potteries in the United States today. In a word, he instituted old world methods to realize the old world effect.

The process of tile making as undertaken here is simple in its primitiveness. The clay, once arriving is composed of the white and dark variety. Both are carefully screened and by a judicious mixture of the white and dark earth, patient drying with practiced firing of the kiln, shades of coloring ranging from pink to black are obtained. After screening and mixing the clay is shoveled into a pit and thoroughly soaked until the consistency of soft putty. From there it is shoveled into a clay mill and the faithful mule goes round and round with the extending arc propelling the clay knives. At the bottom of this clay mill is an aperture through which oozes the clay, greatly refined. It is next piled up and constantly kept moist until ready for the workers on the tables. Here are the forms where the potter thumping his wet clay pats, thumps and cuts with the most primordial of wire contrivances, the clay into the different forms that range along the table. These forms are next placed in the dryers and right there great care must be exercised. It is of great importance that every precaution in the care of shade and sunlight be enforced, otherwise the tile will crack. Before placing in the molds the clay is sanded so the tile will not stick to the molds in the process of drying. The period of drying is dependable on the

A small blue frog sprinkler head. Base 5 3/4 inches by 6 1/4 inches, height 3 1/2 inches. Los Manos Pottery. Circa 1918-1933. Courtesy Boca Raton Historical Society.

weather, usually from three to four days.

The tile, once dried, is next drilled with one small hole at each end to enable means of fastening to the roof. Next comes the kilns, where the tile is piled in and the fires in the ovens started. The opening in the kiln is then tightly sealed with brick and clay, so that not a ray of heat may escape and degree to the 2600 point is reached and maintained for four days and nights. The tile, when through with the kiln, is a finished product and each individual in its shading, as only a hand made tile can be. Proportionate mixture of red and white clay with the handling in kiln, the graduation of heat in the baking produce the desired results.

The case of glazed pottery, urns, vases, garden pots, etc. is followed out along the same identical lines. On their leaving the kilns, they are subject to a coat of glaze applied with a brush and then placed back in the kilns for another baking of the glaze. Symbols, figures, etc.

Large Mizner blue flower pot. Height 24 1/2 inches, base 14 1/2 inches, width 26 inches. Turned upper lip with five incised circumferential lines, four flower-like buttons on base and eight decorative raised buttons about upper lip. Unsigned. Los Manos Pottery. Circa 1918-1933. Courtesy, Boca Raton Historical Society.

A large two handled blue jug decorated with two lions' heads. Height 25 inches, width 13 inches, mouth 8 1/2 inches, base 4 3/4 inches. Marked on base "705" in light blue glaze. Circa 1918-1933. Los Manos Pottery. Courtesy Boca Raton Historical Society.

---

are impressed as in all similar lines by molds, the coloring of the pottery is, of course, done in the glazing.

Today, 20,000 tiles are ready for shipment across the lake. The three kilns, one of 10,000 capacity, one of 3,000 and the third intended for the use of pottery only, accommodating 300 tiles, were all in full operation and doing their bit to help the roofs of the Paris Singer Colony (The Everglades Club) vie with the flowers in the strivings of Mr. Mizner for fragrance and flowers, beauty and memories. (4)

Mizner became a student of ceramic manufacture with notes on plant management, cost accounting, air conditioning, warping and shrinkable, delayed crazing, chemical preparations for different glaze colors, firing and even fireproofing.(5)

Addison Mizner and Mizner Industries, which included the Pottery, prospered. The net worth of the company listed in the prospectus for the years 1923 to 1929 were:

Year	Net Worth	Profits	%
1923	$54,000	$5,000	9
1924	$63,000	$22,000	35
1925	$170,000	$152,000 (a)	89
1926	$143,000	Loss $27,000 (b)	-
1927	$181,000	$38,000	21
1928	$245,000	$64,000	26
1929	$262,000	$17,000	6
Average	$160,000	$39,000	24

(a) After deducting bad debts of $150,000
(b)After deducting bad debts of $96,000

Small blue daisy vase with yellow inserted flower holder. Base 2 3/4 inches, mouth 3 3/8 inches, height 3 inches. Blue glaze with faint vertical dark blue streaks. Los Manos Pottery. Circa 1918-1933. Unsigned. Courtesy Boca Raton Historical Society.

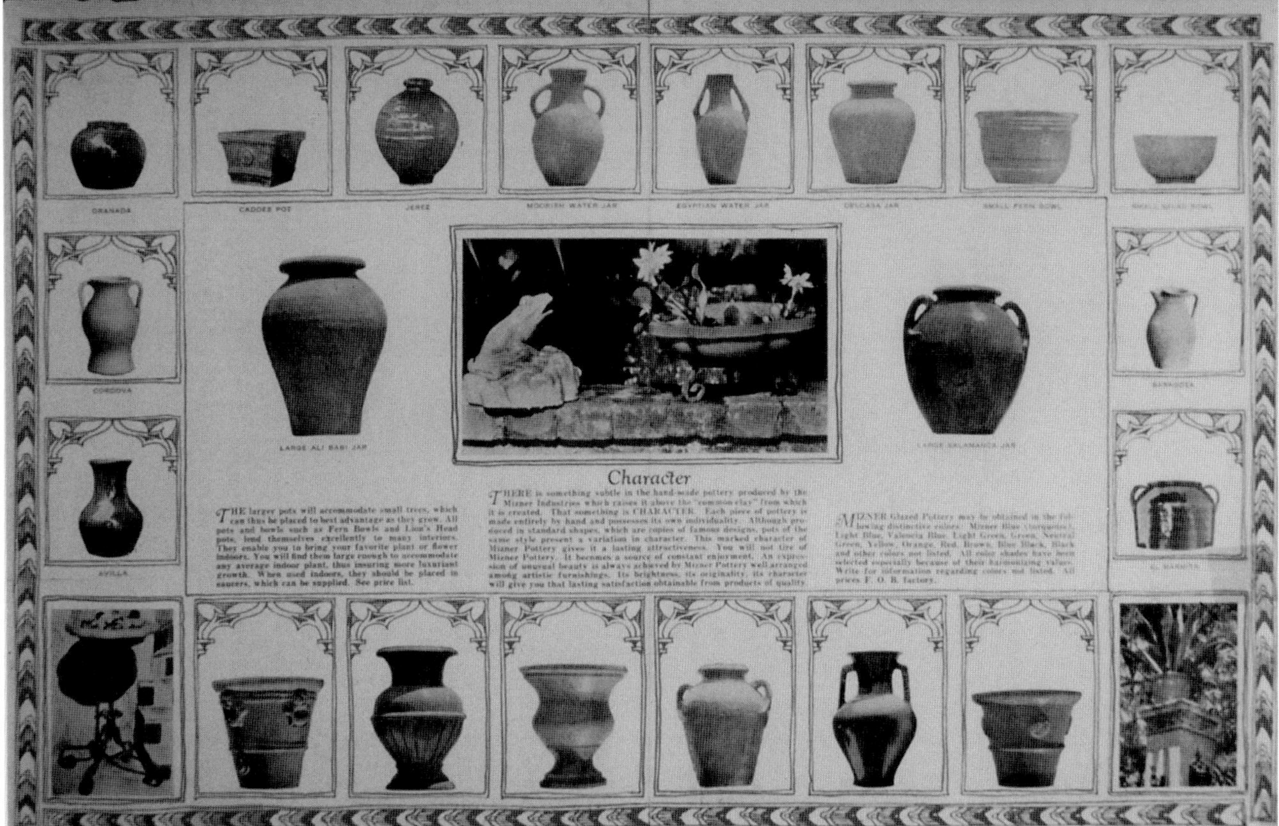

Los Manos Pottery brochure with pictures of different pottery shapes available. Courtesy Historical Society of Palm Beach County.

Mizner went on to begin the development of Boca Raton but the collapse of the Florida land boom in 1925, the Hurricane of 1928 and the collapse of the stock market in 1929 all led to a heart attack and Mizner's death on February 5, 1933. Just before his death, his brother Wilson wired from Hollywood, California, "Stop dying. Am trying to write a comedy." Mizner's answer was typical of his optimistic view of life, "Am going to get well. The comedy goes on."

Mizner was soon forgotten but today Florida's fabulous architect potter is remembered as one of the greatest architects of his time. Few know of his role in Florida pottery.

Base of the yellow and green glazed bowl with the Los Manos Pottery mark. Courtesy Boca Raton Historical Society.

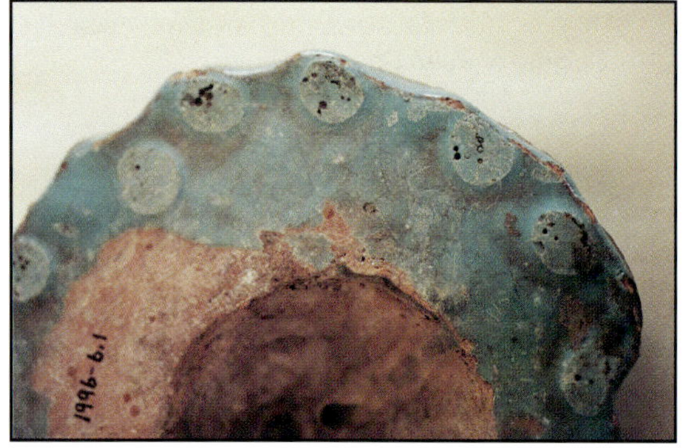

Glaze on the base of many Mizner pots stuck to whatever they were stacked on, producing the puddling and blistering seen here.

Base of the blue lion's head jug with the glazed mark, "705." Courtesy Boca Raton Historical Society.

IDENTIFICATION

Los Manos Pottery was made in sizes ranging from three to four inches in height to pots capable of holding small trees. Mizner Glazed Pottery was obtainable in many distinctive colors including Mizner Blue (turquoise), light blue, valencia blue, light green, green, neutral green, yellow, orange, red, brown, blue black, black and other colors.

The small pots were thrown on a wheel but the larger pots are made as follows:

> To make large cast stone pots, establish a pipe in the ground on a flat surface, make a sweep or template the shape of the inside mole or form for the pot, place a quantity of wet sand around the pipe and make a sand form, using the sweep to shape it...the sweep being made to form this mold; then apply a neet cement to the outside of the form to harden it. After this has set it is used as a core, then apply a separating material, then a layer of cement of plaster. Over this lay plenty of reinforcing wire, then apply plenty of cement plaster on it and finish the outside with another sweep or template which forms the outside of the pot. (5)

Red Georgia clay was used on wheel thrown pottery and a concrete mix on the larger pieces. Glaze was applied thickly and over the years has flaked off unevenly on some examples.

Mizner produced typical Spanish styled pots with characteristic shapes illustrated here in the Los Manos Pottery brochure and in archival photographs found at the Historical Society of Palm Beach County.

Los Manos pottery is frequently found stamped on the base, "LOS MANOS POTTERY, HAND MADE, PALM BEACH, FLA."

Unmarked pottery can be identified by referring to shapes illustrated in the Los Manos brochure. A characteristic finding on both signed and unsigned pottery is the puddling and blistering of the thick flat glaze on the base of pottery from stacking in the kiln.

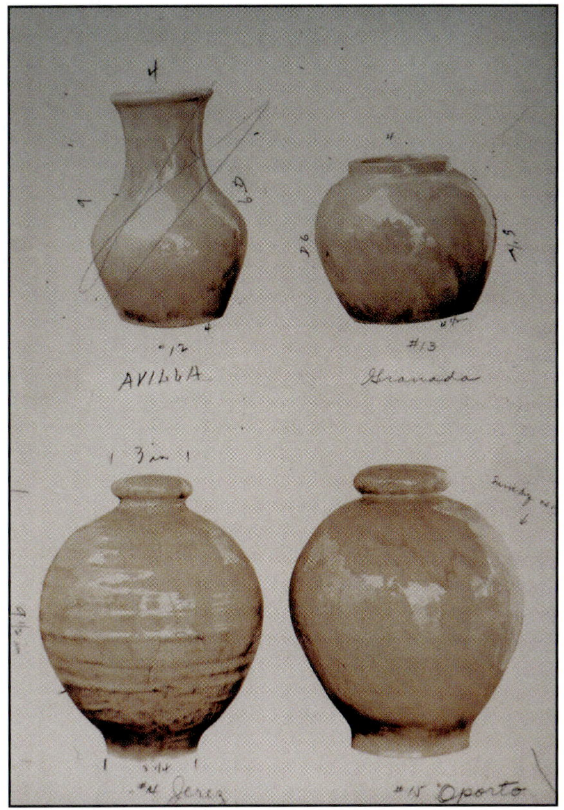

Photographs from the Los Manos Pottery file illustrating different pottery designs and sizes. Courtesy, Historical Society of Palm Beach County.

Chapter Eight

Joseph A. Kohler, Kohler Ware Florida Pottery, St. Petersburg, Florida. Circa 1920-1931.

Kohler Ware Florida Pottery
St. Petersburg, Florida
1920-1931

Joseph A. Kohler, one of the four sons of John W. Kohler, founder of the Southern Pottery Works, grew up in Pensacola and for 15 years learned the pottery business from his father. As a young man he moved to Jacksonville where he met Blanche K. Knight of Daytona. They were married on December 29, 1901 and sometime later moved to St. Petersburg where they lived at Tangerine Avenue near Pine Lawn. (1) The first listing for the pottery at "24th near Euclid Blvd." (today 38th Avenue North) appears in the 1920 City Directory.

It's likely that John W. Kohler was living with his son in St. Petersburg until shortly before his death in 1916, when he returned to Pensacola. Joe Kohler was an independent, tough sort of man who did whatever it took to make a living. A master carpenter, he traveled about the state, frequently with his family, doing construction work from Belle Glade and Pahokee to Wachula.

The first public notice of Joe Kohler's pottery appeared in the *St. Petersburg Daily Times* on the morning of February 4, 1920, and reads in part:

> Pinellas Fair Opens with Fine Displays, Exhibits in Every Department Ahead of Any Previous Show and Big Crowds Expected to Visit Largo to See Them…A beautiful display of small articles of hand painted pottery forms one of the attractive displays in the Art Department. This work is turned out by the Kohler Pottery at St. Petersburg.

Kohler sold his ware directly from his shop and through retail souvenir shops. An ad in the *St. Petersburg Daily Times*, February 7, 1920, for The Curio at 233 Central Avenue, advertised:

Mammy dolls hand made from pine needles, hand painted Florida orange blossom china, The Kohler Line pottery vases, the A.B. Commons Line of Brooches (the work of an artist) and live alligators and porcupine fish mounted while you wait.

Kohler was an active member of the St. Petersburg business community and in 1922 contributed to a publicity campaign to advertise the city. The first official announcement of the opening of Kohler's pottery appeared in the November 12, 1930 edition of the *St. Petersburg Times*.

POTTERY COMPANY OPENS PLANT HERE. Under the management of Mr. And Mrs. J. A. Kohler, St. Petersburg has added another to its already large list of small industries with the opening of the Florida Pottery at 2462 and 2466 Central Avenue.

A vase decorated with blue bird, palm and beach. Stamped on base, "KOHLER ART POTTERY, ST PETERSBURG, FLORIDA." Circa 1920-1931. Courtesy of Jim Blanchard, Jacksonville, Florida.

A group of four vases, three with Egyptian decoration and one with flowers. None signed or stamped "Kohler," but all from the Kohler family and decorated by Mr. Copson, who worked at the Kohler pottery, as gifts for the family. The chariot vase 7 1/4 inches high, Oblelisk, 8 1/2 inches, pitcher with three figures 11 1/2 inches high and the flower vase 10 inches high. Kohler Art Pottery, St. Petersburg, Florida. Circa 1920-1931. Courtesy of Alvin Kohler.

A vase decorated with oranges and branch, typical swirled red orange clay with darker red brown swirls. Seven and one-quarter inches high, 3 1/4 inches wide. Stamped on base, "KOHLER ART POTTERY, ST. PETERSBURG, FLORIDA." Circa 1920-1931.

With its business the manufacture of pottery of all kinds, the new concern is turning out an exclusively Floridian product. The raw clay used to manufacture the many articles made by this concern comes from a county of West Florida, and is processed and made into completed products in the company's plant in this city.

Kohler learned his business from his father and has more than fifteen years of working experience at his trade. According to Mr. Kohler, the clay in its raw condition is found in the state in five natural colors.

The reason for the delay of ten years in formally announcing the opening of the Kohler Pottery may have had something to do with the onset of the Depression, little construction work and Kohler's need to earn a living.

In 1931 Kohler received an offer from Royal H. Carlock, a "Pictorial Artist Photographer, Subjects of Historical Interest" to come to Washington, D.C. and make pottery for him. Carlock offered to pay half of the expenses to Washington, "so we can talk and look over the clay…I can assure you of permanent and profitable employment…I am satisfied that I could put such a line as yours across but it would take time…there is another man in Carolina that wishes to open up here for me but I believe your craftsmanship and imagination is superior to his."(3) Kohler stayed in St. Petersburg.

Mr. Copson, an English artist who worked at the Manatee and Graack Potteries, was a friend and neighbor of Kohler's and the family has a number of special vases signed and decorated by him as presents for the children. Kohler Ware pottery is quite rare in spite of the fact that it was produced from 1920 to 1931.

Joseph Kohler died in 1942 and is buried with his wife Blanche, in the small Sunny Side Cemetery on 54th Avenue North in St. Petersburg, across from Northeast High School and one block east of I-275. His grave is marked with two large Kohler clay pots! Today, the busy rush of students and travelers passing by are completely oblivious to the last resting place of a unique Florida pottery pioneer.

A vase decorated with oranges and orange branch and accentu-
ated with swirling pattern of clay. Height 11 3/4 inches and 4
inches in diameter at base. Unmarked. Attributed to Kohler Ware
Florida Pottery, St. Petersburg, Florida. Circa 1920-1931.

The Kohler Ware Florida Pottery on what is today 38th Avenue North in St. Petersburg. Circa 1930.

IDENTIFICATION

Kohler Ware Florida Pottery is similar in appearance to Manatee River, Graack and Orlando pottery. Kohler pottery was unglazed on the outside with a clear waterproofing interior glaze. The total of seven known examples are decorated with Florida and Egyptian scenes. Of the two known Kohler pieces stamped on the base, KOHLER ART POTTERY, ST. PETERSBURG, FLORIDA (page 93, 94) one has a few twisting strands of gray, pink or green clay through the body of the pot and the other is plain. A photograph in John H. Kohler's THE POTTER AND THE CLAY, *Florida on the Gulf,* December, 1925 also pictures a swirled pattern of clay on a small vase, presumably from his brother Joe's, Kohler Ware. The attribution of the orange blossom decorated vase on page 96 is based on this picture and the vase on page 95.

Kohler Ware Florida pottery can be identified by:
1) base stamped KOHLER ART POTTERY, ST. PETERSBURG, FLORIDA;
2) the finding of a few twisted strand of mixed color clay in the body of the pot.

Chapter Nine

John W. Crary II

Crary Pottery
Bluff Springs, Florida
1933-1939

The stock market crash of 1929 marked the on-set of the Depression. Factories producing food containers closed and decorative pottery was not in demand. People were without jobs or money but in northern Florida, southern Alabama and southern Georgia they still needed to preserve their foods. The Depression, a wandering hobo and $4.50 were the motivating forces behind the creation of the Crary Pottery at Bluff Springs, Florida.

Bluff Springs, located on State Road 29 an hour's drive north of Pensacola and just five miles south of the Alabama border, is as far as you can get from main stream Florida and still be in the state. Bluff Springs was founded by John Williamson Crary I, who moved to Pensacola from Cincinnati, Ohio in 1857. Crary managed the brick making company of Bacon and Abercrombie in Pensacola where he produced millions of bricks used for the building of Ft. Taylor in Key West and Ft. Jefferson in the Dry Tortugas. Crary invented and patented the first brick manufacturing machine in 1858 and today is recognized as one of the pioneers of the brick manu-facturing industry in the United States. Crary had Bluff Springs platted, laid out the streets and parks, built some homes and named his city for the nearby series of small springs at the foot of bluffs along the west shore of the Escambia River separating Escambia from Santa Rosa county. The Civil War ended development, but Crary built a brick busi-ness on the land and ran it with his son John W. Crary II until his death in 1897. (2)

In 1933 John Crary II and his two sons John W. Crary III and Martin Crary were, like most Ameri-cans, suffering through the Depression. They were running a general store in Bluff Springs. With little cash coming in another source of income was needed.

John Williamson Crary II (1862-1933) one of the founders of the Crary Pottery. Crary is sitting in front of an "oil house". In the distance, on the left behind the oil house is Crary's Mill where, according to Don Fredgant, the pottery was located. A 10X glass on the original brings out, "MEAL, GRITS, CORN SHELLED, CRACKED CORN."

Don Fredgant is the source of the only surviving interview with the Crarys. Fredgant indicates that a Mr. Pylant, an itinerant potter from Prattville, Alabama, came to the Crary home and suggested the family try pottery making. He estimated that several thousand dollars would be needed to start up a pottery. The Crarys used bricks from the old family brick yard, closed for three decades, to build a kiln. A gasoline powered pug mill was used for mixing the clay and a hand made potters wheel for turning. The Crarys spent $4.50 for some metal turn-ings and were in the pottery business. (3)

Pylant, or Pie as he was called, was the first pot-ter working for the Crarys. Fredgant indicates that two other potters worked at Bluff Springs. Ralph Phillips from Rock Mills, Alabama, who had learned his pottery skills from his father and Jarvan Brown, the brother of Davis P. Brown, a well known North Carolina potter. Jarvan Brown moved his family to Bluff Springs from Forest Park, Georgia in 1934.

The first kiln was built in a simple rectangular shape, but in 1934, Davis Brown came down from North Carolina and helped build a round, domed kiln with six fire doors and five chimneys. The kiln was fired with local black jack oak. The Crary family indicates that at the first burning of the kiln, Martin Crary lifted a pot out of the kiln and his father, John W. Crary II, was so excited that he had a heart attack and died shortly thereafter.

The Crarys produced pottery typical of that produced throughout the south, including crocks, churns, storage jugs, pitchers, vases, chicken feeders and roach traps. Fredgant quotes Martin Crary as stating, "If it was made out of pottery, we made it ...and if we didn't make it, it was because we didn't know it could be made out of pottery."

The Crarys sold their ware at a roadside stand on Route 29 in front of the pottery and across the road from the family home. Crary traveled throughout the South selling his ware. Don Fredgant quotes Martin Crary:

"I went all the way over to the Alabama-Mississippi line, up to south of Birmingham, across to Atlanta, down to Havana (near Tallahassee) and then home. I'd load up a truck with pottery and leave with it. I tried packing it with excelsior to cushion the pieces , but there was alot of breakage.

A display of pottery for sale at the Crary Pottery on Route 29 in Bluff Springs, Florida. The timber building was converted to a pottery from a general store or gas station. The brick structure at the far left may be a kiln. Circa 1933-1939

A roadside stand displaying Crary clay sculpture that may have been for sale at the pottery.

Finally, I would just load it up tight, draw the sides together with rope, and use a wrench to tighten it all up so nothing would move around."

According to Fredgant the Crary potters were paid on a piece work basis, at the rate of 9 cents per gallon of wares out of the kiln. Little was wasted. Crary remembered only two kiln loads in over five years that were lost through misfiring. The Crarys would pay their turners 9 cents a gallon or 36 cents for a four gallon churn. Crary wholesaled the pottery at 12 1/2 cents a gallon or 50 cents for a four gallon churn; store owners would retail the same piece for 75 cents to a dollar.

By 1939 the Depression was ending and cheap mass produced pottery had come back into the market and forced the Crarys out of business.

"It got so we couldn't compete anymore," said Martin Crary as quoted by Don Fredgant. "When we quit there were truck and trailer loads of pottery coming down from Ohio, Kentucky and Indiana. They were wholesaling it for less than we paid our potters to make it."

Today a trip to Bluff Springs and the Crary home finds things much as they were back in the early 1930s. It's easy to miss the house which sits well back off the highway. The roadside stand and the kiln are gone but out in the barn sit rows of Crary Pottery neatly placed there by the Crarys after the pottery closed in 1939, patiently waiting for the market in Florida Depression pottery to improve.

A five-gallon crock in Albany and Bristol glaze marked with the Crary stamp. Height 12 1/2 inches. Crary Pottery, Bluff Springs, Florida. Circa 1933-1939. Courtesy Mrs. Dean Crary and the Crary family.

A Crary Pottery chicken waterer. Albany glaze. height 12 3/4 inches, width of base 13 inches, height 2 3/4 inches. Unmarked. Crary Pottery, Bluff Springs, Florida. Circa 1933-1939. Courtesy Mrs. Dean Crary and the Crary family.

A four gallon Crary Pottery storage jar with two handles and impressed, CRARY POTTERY, BLUFF SPRINGS, FLA. 4. The turned lip is unglazed to permit stacking in the kiln, a Georgia pottery tradition. The top half covered with a brown Albany slip glaze which has run into the lower clear glaze giving the effect of a gold band about the waist. Height 15 1/2 inches, base diameter 8 3/4 inches. Circa 1933-1939.

A Crary Pottery ten gallon stoneware storage jar with two applied handles the ends of both tapered and fixed to the side of the jar with thumb, index and middle finger. The rim unglazed to permit stacking in the kiln, a Georgia pottery tradition. The top half covered with dark chocolate brown Albany slip glaze running into the clear lower glaze giving the effect of a gold band about the waist. Height 19 inches, base diameter 12 1/4 inches. Impressed CRARY POTTERY, BLUFF SPRINGS, FLA. 10. circa 1933-1939.

IDENTIFICATION

Crary Pottery was made from a red clay dug near Jay, Florida on the Santa Rosa County side of the Escambia River. Three types are found:

glazed inside and out, the most common
glazed inside only
unglazed

Glazes included a chocolate brown Albany slip and a cream colored Bristol glaze. In some cases the glazes must have been mixed to give a light brown or red brown finish. A black glaze was used only on cups, mugs and bowls. Fredgant reports that Martin Crary paid Evan Brown $25.00 for the formula to a "crazy glaze" consisting of a combination of blue, pink, purple and brown against a light background.

The gold band noted around the waist of a number of the illustrated stoneware jars is a feature of Crary Pottery resulting from the application of a chocolate brown glaze to the upper half of a pot and clear glaze to the lower half. During firing the dark glaze bleeds into the clear glaze, giving the effect of a gold band about the middle of the pot.

A possibly unique feature of Crary Pottery is

A Crary pot in a mixed glaze. height 14 1/4 inches. Unmarked. Crary Pottery, Bluff Springs, Florida. Circa 1933-1939. Courtesy Mrs. Dean Crary and the Crary family.

A Crary Pottery stoneware pitcher, dark chocolate brown glaze. Applied handle with end shaped with thumb, index and middle fingers. Impressed, CRARY POTTERY, BLUFF SPRINGS, FLA. on side. Height 6 1/2 inches, base diameter 4 1/2 inches. Circa 1933-1939.

A one-handled, three gallon Crary churn. mixed Albany and bristol glazes. height 14 1/2 inches. Unmarked. Crary Pottery, Bluff Springs, Florida. Circa 1933-1939. Courtesy Mrs. Dean Crary and the Crary family.

A Crary Pottery single handled, two gallon storage jar. Unglazed upper lip to permit stacking in the kiln, a Georgia pottery tradition. Impressed CRARY POTTERY, BLUFF SPRINGS, FLA. 2, on side. Top half covered with a brown Albany slip glaze which has run into the lower clear glaze giving the effect of a gold band about the waist. Height 12 inches, base diameter 8 inches. Circa 1933-1939.

A Crary Pottery three gallon stoneware storage jar with two handles the end of one fixed to side with thumb, middle and index fingers. Turned lip and incised line below lip. Tan glaze. Impressed, CRARY POTTERY, BLUFF SPRINGS, FLA. 3, on side. Height 13 1/2 inches, base diameter 8 1/2 inches. Circa 1933-1939.

the design and attachment of the handle to the side of a storage vessel. Most handles seen in southern pottery have a tapered handle, a rat tail handle or single or double thumb print handles. The Crary's used the thumb, index and middle fingers, held together, to attach the lower part of the handle to the body, resulting in a triple indentation matching these three fingers.

The Crarys never considered it important to stamp or sign their pots but many pieces can be found with an impressed stamp mark that reads, CRARY POTTERY/ BLUFF SPRINGS/ FLA.

A yellow glazed, four-gallon churn with lug handle and regular handle. Height 16 1/4 inches. Unmarked. Crary Pottery, Bluff Springs, Florida. Circa 1933-1939. Courtesy Mrs. Dean Crary and the Crary family.

An umbrella stand shaped pot. Unglazed outside. Albany slip inside. height 24 1/2 inches. Unmarked. Crary Pottery, Bluff Springs, Florida. Circa 1933-1939. Courtesy Mrs. Dean Crary and the Crary family.

A Crary Pottery water jug. Earthenware. Circa 1933-1939. Unglazed outside, clear glaze inside. Height 9 1/4 inches, base diameter 4 inches. Impressed, CRARY POTTERY, BLUFF SPRINGS, FLA. on base.

A large two-handled storage jar in Albany glaze. height 21 3/4 inches,
Unmarked. Crary Pottery, Bluff Springs, Florida. Circa 1933-1939.
Courtesy Mrs. Dean Crary and the Crary family.

Chapter Ten

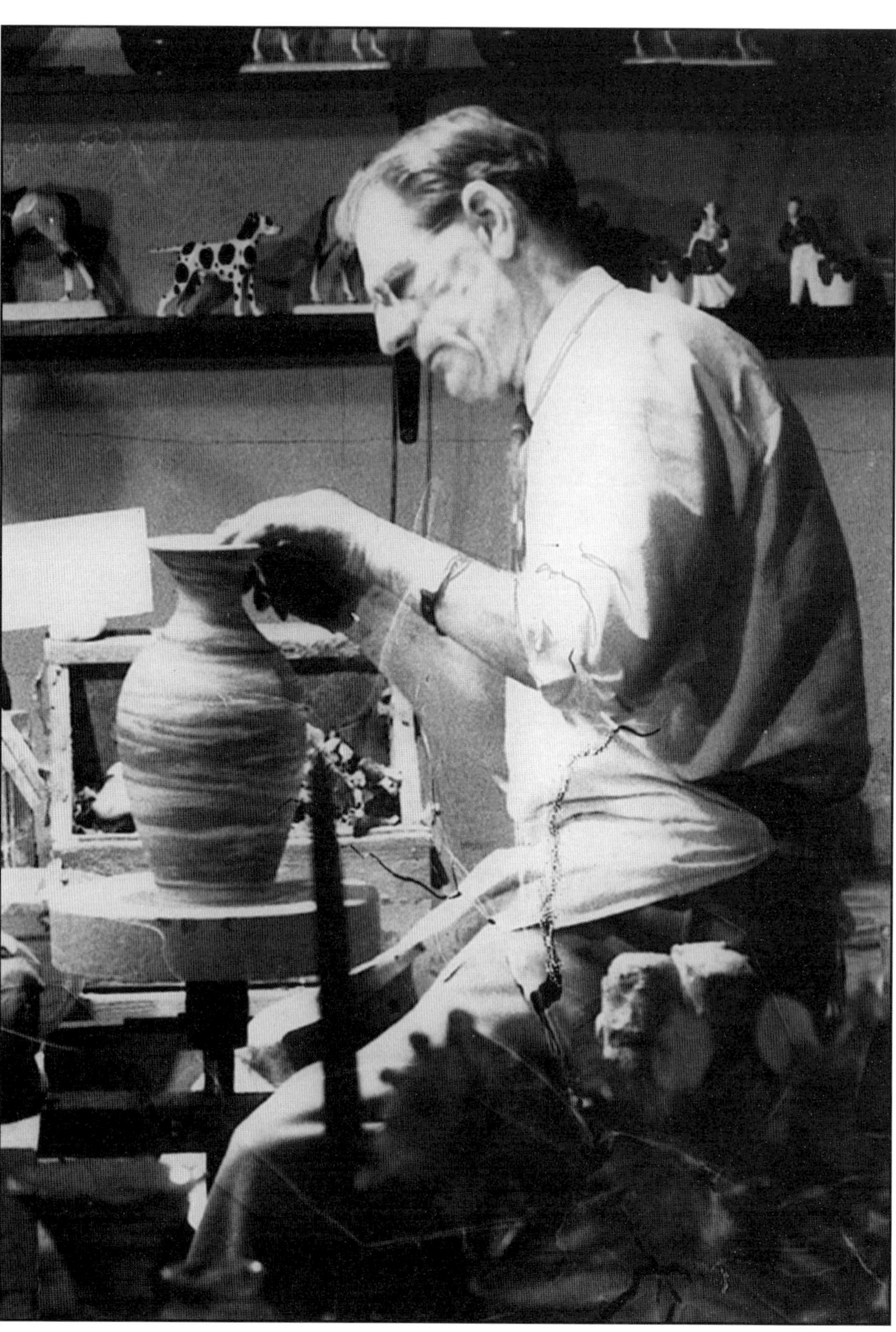

Henry Graack at the wheel. Silver Springs, Florida. Circa 1935-1966

Silver Springs Pottery
Ocala, Florida
1935-1966

The Graacks left Bradentown sometime in 1924. The senior Graack returned to his home in Kolding, Denmark and Henry Graack Jr. moved to New York City where he worked in a brickyard. Graack met a young woman, Albina Hanke and they were married. In 1927 a daughter, Madelyn, was born.(1)

Conversations with Mr. Pell, the owner of the Fort Ticonderoga Attraction in Ticonderoga, New York, led to a job at the fort making copies of early Indian pottery. Soon Graack was making pottery for sale to the summer tourists visiting the fort on upper Lake George.

An earthenware double handled jug and an earthenware double handled bowl, both made by Henry Graack to simulate early indian pottery. The jug 7 1/2 inches high and the bowl 5 inches high. Ink stamped on base, FORT TICONDEROGA, NEW YORK. U.S.A. Fort Ticonderoga Pottery, Fort Ticonderoga, New York. Circa 1930-1966.

Sometime after he began working at the fort, Graack met with William Rae, the owner of Silver Springs in Ocala, Florida, and agreed to open a pottery concession at the Spring. In 1935 the Graack

family moved to Ocala. Sitting out in the warm Florida sun was a pleasant change from the bitter winters of upstate New York.

William B. Rae, the son of Willliam Rae, was seven years old when the Graacks moved to Ocala. He remembers Henry Graack as a quiet but likable man, with thick glasses, pale skin and with hands that were dry and cracked from kneading wet clay. Rae remembers throwing a rock into the spring. Graack told him to stop because, "if everyone did that they'd fill the spring up!" (2)

The Silver Springs pottery sat just back from the main spring where the glass bottomed boats were docked. The pottery was located next to a novelty and gift shop, Barber Groves, orange packers who also sold ice cream and Cokes, Scudder's Antique

A large unglazed vase with green, red and white swirls. Impressed on base, "Fort Ticonderoga". Price penciled on base, $2.00. Height 8 inches, mouth 5 1/4 inches, base 3 3/4 inches. Fort Ticonderoga Pottery, Ft. Ticonderoga, New York. Circa1930-1966.

Silver Springs Pottery workshop at Silver Springs, Florida. Circa 1935-1966

shop, the Ross Allen Florida Reptile Institute and Tooey's Jungle Cruises. The Silver Springs of 1935-1955 was a lot different than it is today. People were more relaxed. Today the spring is closed to swimmers but then you could lie on the beach next to the spring, go for a swim or watch a potter at his wheel.

The pottery shop had a large sign overhead that read "WATCH the POTTER at WORK." Henry Graack would sit out in front of his shop, sometimes surrounded by 15 to 20 people, turning his wheel, shaping his clay and talking to the tourists.

Graack obtained his clay from a mine near Gainesville. The pottery was air dried for a few days and then placed in a kiln at 2000 to 2500 degrees Fahrenheit. Graack produced what would sell. Small (3-4 inches) unglazed pieces with swirling flat pink and green colors were most popular and sold for $1.00 to $2.00. Glazed pansy pitchers were also popular, especially when stuffed with wildflowers that grew at the spring. Larger pieces, including pitchers. teapots, bowls and plates, were made, both glazed and unglazed. All pottery was stamped, SILVER SPRINGS, FLA. and the larger, more attractive pieces, signed by the potter, *H. A.*

A glazed teapot 8 1/2 inches high and 8 inches wide with two rows of circumferential incised lines about the upper body and applied rope handle. Stamped on base, SILVER SPRINGS, FLA. and signed, "GRAACK". Silver Springs Pottery, Ocala, Florida. Circa 1935-1966.

Henry Graack turning a small vessel for Mr. Ripley of "Ripley's Believe It or Not."

Graack. Each morning some of the pottery was scented with orange blossoms.

Al Scudder was a small boy who grew up in Ocala. His mother ran Scudders Antiques at the Spring. He remembers watching Henry Graack pushing his treadle wheel and turning pottery. He describes Graack as a quiet, friendly man who was physically strong in appearance. He remembers Graack placing his finished pottery on a 1 X 8 board to dry in the sun and at the end of the day lifting the board heavy with pottery onto his shoulder. He then carried his work about 300 yards back to his kiln, which was located behind the bath houses. (3)

World War II began and in 1942 tourism stopped and the pottery shop closed. Graack worked briefly at a pottery in Zanesville, Ohio learning to make pottery molds.(1) After the war, the pottery at Silver Springs opened again.

Graack continued to make his colorful pottery, in the summer at Fort Ticonderoga, and in the winter, at Silver Springs. Young Madelyn Graack found the moves back and forth caused problems with her school work. The Ocala City Directory for 1947 lists Madelyn as a "student." Henry Graack wanted his daughter to learn the potter's skills and become the fourth generation of Graacks producing pottery. Madelyn, however, vigorously resisted and instead married a young man, Pete Peterson. A native of Ocala, Peterson was working part time as an assistant at the pottery while studying economics at the University of Florida.

After 31 years of work at Silver Springs, during which time he produced a large legacy of beautiful Florida pottery, Henry A. Graack died in Ocala on September 20, 1966. In a few years Albina moved to St., Mary's, Georgia to live with her daughter. She died there in 1982. Madelyn had two children and currently is retired and living in Florida with her husband.

A glazed pitcher with applied handle. Height 5 inches width 7 1/2 inches. Stamped., SILVER SPRINGS, FLA. H.A. GRAACK, POTTER." Circa 1935-1966.

A green and brown glazed cream pitcher, signed on base, "GRAACK" and stamped SILVER SPRINGS, FLA. Height 3 inches, base 1 3/4 inches, mouth 2 3/4 inches. Silver Springs Pottery, Ocala, Florida. Circa1935-1966.

A pot with lid and geometric painted decorations. Height 9 inches, mouth 5 inches and base 4 1/2 inches. Impressed on base, "Ft. Ticonderoga Pottery, FT. Ticonderoga, New York. Circa 1930-1966. Courtesy of Jim Blanchard, Jacksonville, Florida.

A bud vase with black, purple and yellow swirls and small holes around the mouth. Signed on the base, "Potter" with a wide H and A above the H and G below the H and stamped SILVER SPRINGS, FLA. Height 2 inches, width at the waist 3 inches. Silver Springs Pottery, Ocala, Florida. Circa 1935-1966.

A glazed multicolored vase with a cream colored interior glaze. Signed with a series of dots, "Graack" and stamped SILVER SPRINGS, FLA. Silver Springs Pottery, Ocala Florida. Circa 1935-1966

A glazed bowl with swirling green, black and brown colors. Height 6 inches, width 5 inches. Stamped "SILVER SPRINGS, FLA." and signed, "GRAACK." Circa 1935-1966.

A glazed vase 3 3/4 inches high and 3 3/4 inches wide. Stamped, SILVER SPRINGS, FLA. and signed, "GRAACK." Silver Springs Pottery, Ocala, Florida. Circa 1935-1966.

A pink, gray and charcoal colored vase, unglazed outside and clear glaze inside. Multiple circumferential grooves turned into the body of vase. Stamped,. "SILVER SPRINGS, FLA." and signed with a series of dots, "GRAACK." Height 4 3/4 inches, mouth 2 1/2 inches and base 2 inches. Silver Springs Pottery, Ocala, Florida. Circa 1935-1966.

A multi colored unglazed vase in green, pink and white. Incised turning line around the neck. Height 6 inches, width at waist 4 inches. Hand printed, twice, on the base, SILVER SPRINGS, FLA. Silver Springs Pottery, Ocala, Florida. Circa 1935-1966.

A vase unglazed outside, white glaze inside. Signed with a series of dots, "graack" and stamped, "SILVER SPRINGS. FLA". Height 6 1/2 inches, mouth 3 1/2 inches, base 2 1/2 inches. Silver Springs Pottery, Ocala, Florida. Circa 1935-1966.

A multi colored vase unglazed exterior, brown glaze interior. Signed on the base twice with hand printing, SILVER SPRINGS, FLA. Height 5 3/4 inches, mouth 3 1/2 inches. base 2 1/2 inches. Silver Springs Pottery, Ocala, Florida, Circa 1935-1966.

A small unglazed multi colored vase with a cream colored interior glaze. Height 2 3/4 inches, width at the waist 3 1/4 inches. Stamped, "SILVER SPRINGS, FLA." and signed, H, with the A above the H and the G below, potter. Silver Springs Pottery, Ocala, Florida. Circa 1935-1966.

A pink and charcoal vase unglazed outer surface, clear glazed inner. Height 3 1/2 inches width 2 1/2 inches at the waist. Stamped on the base, SILVER SPRINGS, FLA. and signed H, with A above the H and G below. Henry A. Graack, potter. Silver Springs Pottery, Ocala, Florida. Circa 1935-1966.

A Yale blue glazed vase 6 inches wide at waist, 4 1/2 inches high. Inscribed on base, SILVER SPRINGS, FLORIDA. Circa 1935-1966.

An unglazed wide mouthed vase with decorative wavy line incised around the lip. Stamped twice on the base, SILVER SPRINGS, FLA. Height 4 inches, mouth 3 1/2 inches and base 2 1/2 inches. Silver Springs Pottery, Ocala, Florida. Circa 1935-1966.

A group of 2 inch and 3 inch unglazed bud vases, all stamped on the base, SILVER SPRINGS, FLA

A group of 2 inch to 3 inch unglazed Silver Springs Pottery souvenirs. All stamped SILVER SPRINGS, FLA on the base.

A group of 1 inch to 1 1/2 inch unglazed salt and pepper shakers all stamped on the side, SILVER SPRINGS, FLA.

A Yale blue glazed pansy pitcher 6 inches high and 4 1/2 inches wide and a Yale blue glazed vase 6 inches high and 4 1/2 inches wide, both inscribed with hand printing on the base, "SILVER SPRINGS, FLA." The pitcher with "H. A. GRAACK, POTTER" added. Silver Springs Pottery, Ocala, Florida. Circa 1935-1966.

IDENTIFICATION

Pottery produced by Henry Graack at Silver Springs was most commonly small unglazed souvenir pieces two to four inches in height and made of swirling pastel shades of mixed pink, green, black or white clay. The pottery is marked with an impressed stamp, "Silver Springs, Fla." or "Silver Springs." Many clear glazed examples can be found but these are distinctly rarer and found in swirled color combinations of black, pink, purple, white, orange, brown or green. The glazed examples are generally larger and more intricate in design than unglazed pieces. Pitchers, pansy pitchers, teapots and vases were also made. Examples with a Yale Blue glaze exist. The smaller pieces were all stamped "Silver Springs, Fla." and the larger glazed pieces signed "Graack" or "Potter H.A.Graack."

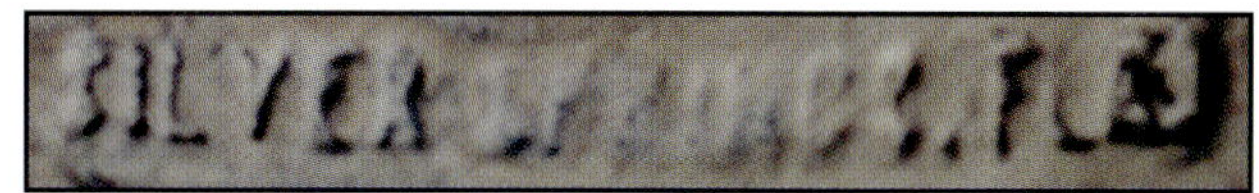

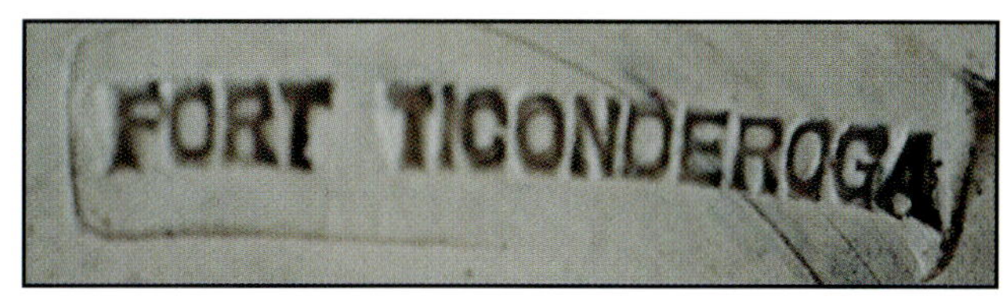

Chapter Eleven

Mel Casper turning a pot at the Merritt Island Pottery.

The Merritt Island Pottery
Merritt Island
1937-1999

It was the birds, the lushness of the vegetation, dreams of growing oranges and hope of starting a pottery that first brought the family to the island. In 1937 Thomas and Esther Jamieson, their adopted son Melvin Casper, and Esther's brother, an ornithologist, left their hectic life in Chicago for the beauty and quiet of Merritt Island. The island, located between the Indian and Banana Rivers near Cocoa, was still a wilderness. Thomas, in poor health, was a retired high school principal and Esther, or Peggy as she preferred to be called, was a noted sculptress. Their stepson Melvin, now 21 years old, had developed an interest in art while in grammar school and had studied for three years at the Art Institute of Chicago. Melvin, in preparation for the work he wanted to do in Florida, also studied with Eugene Deutsch, a well known Chicago potter.

The family purchased an orange grove and a small house on ten acres on the south end of the island. In 1937 there were 9 other people living there. Ospreys, eagles and egrets were everywhere and so were the mosquitoes. There was no electricity and no telephone. Residents carried hand saws in their cars to clear fallen trees off the dirt roads after a storm.

The Jamiesons and young Wilbur cut timber on their property, took it to a lumber mill where it was cut into boards and used it to expand the existing house and build a small pottery. Peggy Jamieson and Melvin Casper, mother and son, founded the Merritt Island Pottery. The location of the pottery, on a nearly deserted island, may seem strange but many successful potteries were located at a distance from a ready market.

In the beginning things were tough. There were problems getting clay in Florida in small enough

A hurricane lamp base 4 1/2 inches high, shade 9 1/2 inches. Marked on bisque parts of base and shade, "Merritt Island potters." Base also with torn paper label that reads in part, "Tag for item one, Melvin H...RSD 3 Box Merritt Island, Hurricane...Eastern..." Merritt Island Pottery, Merritt Island, Florida. Circa 1937-1999. Courtesy of Jim Blanchard, Jacksonville, Florida.

quantities to make it worthwhile to the sellers and eventually clay was brought in from Tennessee by the carload. There was no power.

For two years we made sculpture and pottery items without having a place to fire them. When we finally did get electricity, we had to buy the poles ourselves.

The first load of pottery they put in their newly fired kiln turned out with an unusual but interesting pox.

A visitor to the shop liked it so well that she bought the entire load.(1)

Casper remembers the visitor well. She arrived in a chaffeur driven car and bought everything. They were disappointed to lose their experimental work with new glazes but they needed the money. By

A large platter or charger with mixed blue and gold glazes, 2 1/2 inches deep and 19 1/2 inches wide. Marked on base, "Merritt Island Potters."

Merritt Island Pottery, Meritt Island, Florida.

Peggy Jamieson with Wilber Casper working at the Merritt Island Pottery.

1940 the pottery was becoming a success. A story in the January 6th issue of the Brevard County edition of the *Miami Herald* announced:

Kentucky Woman Makes Success of Merritt Island Pottery Trade. Peggy Jamieson Brings Fine Sculptural Background Into Work of Shaping Clay Patterns.

When she came to South Merritt Island two years ago and founded the Merritt Island Potteries, Mrs. Jamieson brought with her a sculptural background of natural talent, and capacities for study, hard work and outstanding accomplishment.

Born on a farm in Davis County, Kentucky...she began to display as a child, a talent for the art that has become her life work—barely escaping "many a licking" for grinding up clay from the river in a coffee grinder to provide material for her early attempts at modeling the animals and people about the farm.

Farming for two years and working, during spare moments at her art failed to extinguish...the flame of genius which, she says today, is one per cent talent and 99 per cent hard work.

She attended the Art Institute of Chicago, and finally became associated with Roal Josset, the widely known French sculptor, as a fellow worker and teacher, assisting him in the execution of such commissions as the figure of Washington on the Federal building at the Chicago World's Fair.

"I liked Florida." says Mrs. Jamieson, "because it is so colorful; because the possibilities in almost any line of artistic endeavor seem almost unlimited. There are trees and vegetation in such abundance and variety and there are so many species of animal-everything, almost, seems to lend itself to our medium of artistic expression.

Mrs. Jamieson...and her partner, Melvin Casper, ...create garden pieces, especially designed pots, cooking ware, walking and fireplace tiles, ornamental bas reliefs for mantles, horses, statues and almost every conceivable novelty that may be fashioned from clay. But that beaten path to her door—11 miles from Cocoa, over a road that, for half the distance at least, doesn't afford a great deal of riding pleasure, and her reluctant admission that she "just can't keep any stock," bespeaks plainer than words the fact that the Chicago sculptress has "been discovered"—that she has resumed her career.(2)

One of the first commissions the pottery had was from the Seminole Indian Tribe. The Seminoles wanted to sell pottery to tourists. Casper made several hundred small blank pottery vases and sent them to the Seminoles for hand decoration.(3)

Then came the war. Melvin Casper found himself in the Army and served with General Stillwell in India, China and Burma. Casper helped to teach the Chinese to fight. He was even asked to teach pottery making to patients in a Chinese mental institution but never did. One of his responsibilities was to draw food rations for the Chinese troops. To do this Casper was given a small "Chop Mark" with

A cup with blue, green and brown glaze. Height 4 1/2 inches, mouth 3 1/2 inches and base 2 3/4 inches. Signed on base, Merritt Island Potters. Merritt Island Pottery, Merritt Island, Florida. Circa 1937-1999.

An orange uranium glazed cup. Height 4 1/2 inches, mouth 4 inches, base 3 1/4 inches. Signed on base, Merritt Island Potters. Merritt Island Pottery, Merritt Island, Florida. Circa 1937-1999.

his name carved in the base in Chinese letters. He would use this mark to stamp a receipt for the food. Years later Casper would use this same mark to identify some of his pottery. While her son was away, Peggy Jamieson worked at the nearby Banana River Naval Station.

When the war ended Melvin Casper returned home full of new ideas about pottery inspired by the orient, but it wasn't until July of 1948 that the pottery opened again. Part of the delay in opening was due a post war difficulty in obtaining the needed chemicals for glazes. Casper probably needed time to recuperate as well. When in 1948 the pottery finally did re-open the *Orlando Evening Star* described the work:

> The Merritt Island Potters make broiling plate, baking ware of all kinds, mugs, pitchers, ash trays, chili bowls, cigarette boxes, ornaments and scenic tiles to mention a few of their products. The Brevard Hotel use their marmalade jugs for their dining room. The Chester Groves recently placed a sizable order for selling the Merritt Island products at their highway stand. Instead of Mrs. Jamieson and Mr. Casper having to find wholesale or retail buyers for their wares, the buyers come to them. (4)

A few months later, on March 4, 1949, more than 125 guests were invited to an open house at the pottery. With a local musician, Carl Powell, playing in the background, guests arrived by car or by boat. The *Melbourne Times* advised sailors, "the white pottery workshop with its red roof is directly across river from the radio beach above Plover Pt....Better in an East or Northeast wind for safe anchorage, five feet depth 100 yards off shore. Bring your dinghy."

The *Melbourne Times* describes some of the pottery:

> Two outstanding contemporary pieces,

One of the first commissions the pottery had was from the Seminole Indian Tribe. The Seminoles wanted to sell pottery to tourists. Casper made several hundred small blank pottery vases and sent them to the Seminoles for hand decoration. (3).

An owl like pottery penny bank, 5 inches high and marked on the base, "Merritt Island Potters".

A Chinese New Year figure make at The Merritt Island Pottery. Height 8 inches. Unmarked,

temple dogs with a touch of Ming ancestry, modeled by Peg Jamieson and fired in the flame and copper glaze of uranium ore now tabooed by the government for any commercial use, are worth a motor trip just to see. They are not for sale.

Popular functional pieces of Merritt ware shown at Monday's party were the famous chowder pitcher with two handles, the Tom and Jerry cups, mugs for fruit juice and stronger, casseroles and baking dishes in all sizes from tiny ramekins to family proportions.

Many covered jars had exquisite ceramic flower tops. Colors ran from ming yellow, gulf stream blue to Palmetto and lime green, copper and bronze, richly blended. (5)

By the 1950s the pottery was a busy enterprise with hundreds of people making the trip out to the potters' work. The pottery was on exhibit and for sale at the Island House gift shop.

An advertisement in the *Cocoa Tribune* gives some idea of production at that time.

> There are beautiful enamels that catch the very colors of Florida. Her brilliant skies, her many greens, her hibiscus reds and her white coral sands grace the pins, earrings, bowls and trays....
>
> The pottery is displayed in a richness of color and shapely forms over the entire shop. Useful cooking wares, garden wares, art objects, bowls and pitchers are in plenty.(6)

In April of 1956 Peg Jamieson entered a terra-cotta bull in the fourth annual Miami National Ceramics Exhibition at the Lowe Art Gallery, University of Miami, in Coral Gables. There were over six hundred entries from thirty-two states. These entries were narrowed down to two hundred and fifty for the Miami show. Peg's bull won second prize. (7) (8)

A clear glazed plate, slip decorated with Moravian designs. Made about 1960 by Wilbur Casper for a museum in Salem, North Carolina. Stamped on bottom, OLD SALEM, IN NORTH CAROLINA. Width 10 3/4 inches, height 2 inches. Merritt Island Pottery, Merritt Island, Florida. Circa 1937-1999.

The pottery business continued to expand and Peg and Wilbur were doing well enough to close the pottery for the summer. According to Casper, "We try to go to Europe every second year. The inspiration we find in the potteries and museums over there enables us to come back and sort of renew our own ideas." In 1961 they visited Italy and Germany.

> Business is good—so good that they use ten tons of clay a year in the making of their pieces....and on average make and use two tons of glaze a year. (9)

Everything the pottery made was handmade, molds were rarely used. Once in the case of a gentleman who wanted 50 duplicate Monkeys for garden posts, Peggy carved the monkey out of stone and a mold was made to make the fifty monkey posts. Wilbur remembers someone from Disney asking him to make thousands of plain pottery mugs that would be decorated by Disney. Wilbur refused. The Disney man said, "But you could get a Cadillac!" Wilbur told him he didn't need one.

The pottery was sold to individuals and retailers throughout the country. In 1961 Peggy was quoted by the *Miami Herald.* "We ship more to California, Washington, New York, Massachusetts and the New England states." (10) That year Wilbur, with an entry of a large glazed bowl, won first prize at the Florida State Fair in Tampa.

A yachting magazine printed a story about the Merritt Island Pottery and after that yachts traveling on the intercoastal waterway were pulling over in the Indian River to buy pottery. Again Peggy Jameson, "That's quite a thrill when you see a yacht coming in out there." (11)

The pottery's glazes were developed over years of testing. The uranium glaze, a beautiful orange, was discontinued when the government forbid the use of uranium. Other glazes included Indian River blue, avocado green, palm gray, alligator black and armadillo pink.(12)

Peggy and her son continued to produce unique pottery and both taught two classes a week to local pottery students. In June of 1980 Peggy died at the age of eighty-five. The Brevard Art Center and Museum, in Melbourne, dedicated a room in her memory.

Wilbur Casper continued on in the pottery.

A bowl 14 3/4 inches in diameter. Mixed glaze. Marked, "Merritt Island Potters" on base. Merritt Island Pottery, Merritt Island, Florida. Circa 1937-1999. Courtesy of Jim Blanchard, Jacksonville. Florida.

A small vase in Indian River Blue with Chinese chop mark. Height 4 inches. Marked on base "Merritt Island Potters." Merritt Island Pottery, Merritt Island, Florida. Circa 1937-1999. Courtesy of Jim Blanchard, Jacksonville. Florida.

A blue vase marked on base. "Merritt Island Potters." Height 6 inches. Merritt Island Pottery, Merritt Island, Florida. Circa 1937-1999. Courtesy of Jim Blanchard, Jacksonville. Florida.

The top of a hurricane lamp. Base marked "Merritt Island Potters." Height 9 inches. Merritt Island Pottery, Merritt Island, Florida. Circa 1937-1999. Courtesy of Jim Blanchard, Jacksonville. Florida.

A plate with blue slip chicken design. Marked on back, "Merritt Island Potters." Courtesy of Larry Roberts, Micanopy, Florida.

A plate with tarpon slip decoration. Diameter 9 1/2 inches. Marked on back, "Merritt Island Potters." Courtesy of Larry Roberts, Micanopy, Florida.

A small cup with Chinese chop mark. Three and one-half inches high. Marked, "Merritt Island Potters." Courtesy of Larry Roberts, Micanopy, Florida.

A gold, green and brown mixed glaze bowl with lid. Height 6 inches, width 7 inches. Marked on base, "Merritt Island Potters." Courtesy of Larry Roberts, Micanopy, Florida.

Two small lidded jars and two vases. All marked on base, "Merritt Island Potters." Courtesy of Larry Roberts, Micanopy, Florida.

Cups all marked on base, "Merritt Island Potters," Courtesy of Larry Roberts, Micanopy, Florida.

A large Merritt Island bowl, 14 inches wide and 8 1/2 inches deep. Marked on base, "Merritt Island Potters."

A Merritt Island casserole. Marked on base, "Merritt Island Potters."

A cup with slip decorated fish and a large handle. Height 4 1/2 inches. Marked on base, "Merritt Island Potters." Courtesy of Larry Roberts, Micanopy, Florida.

A cup belonging to Peggy Jamieson of the Merritt Island Pottery, Marked, "PEG" with raised letters on the side and "Merritt Island Potters" on the base. Courtesy of Larry Roberts, Micanopy, Florida.

Today at the age of eighty-three, he continues to make pottery. Over the years a lot has changed on the island but the pottery and the natural beauty around it remain the same. The pottery in 1999 looks much as it did in the 1950s. The same kilns remain, the same potters kickwheel remains but one is electrified. Two days a week students work in a backroom with Wilbur and tourists and locals drop by frequently to purchase pottery and chat with Wilbur.

The Merritt Island Pottery is a remarkable example of studio pottery production in Florida. Amazingly after 62 years, Wilbur Casper remains working there today, a master potter hardened by the fire of World War II and glazed by the quiet and beauty of Merritt Island.

IDENTIFICATION

The Merritt Island Pottery produced a wide range of useful dinner and kitchen ware including plates, bowls, cups, pitchers, pots, casseroles, baking dishes, large mugs and trays. Most of this pottery was slip decorated with fish, flowers or other tropical designs and inscribed on the bisque base, "Merritt Island Potters." Penny savings banks were made in the shape of pigs or owls.

Merritt Island potters made decorative garden

Maker's Mark signed on base of ash tray.

Various stamps used to decorate Merritt Island Pottery.

An Indian River Blue glazed ash tray. Marked "Christmas 1967" and signed on base, Merritt Island Potters. Width 4 7/8 inches, height 1 1/4 inches. Merritt Island Pottery, Merritt Island, Florida. circa 1937-1999.

planters, garden chimes, waterfalls and walking tile. Lamp bases and candle sticks were made as well as ash trays and cigarette boxes and jewelry.

Named glazes include: Uranium glaze, discontinued early, Indian River blue, palm gray, avocado green and armadillo pink.

Decorative pottery was produced in the form of attractive jugs and flasks with a metallic brown or gray green glaze. These were inscribed, "Merritt Island Potters" or marked with an added clay wafer stamped with Peggy Jamieson's or Casper's name in Chinese. When Peggy Jamieson died in 1980 Wilbur began signing his pieces, "Merritt Island Pottery." Large decorative bowls and trays were made with varying glazes. Sculpture in all forms was done including figurines, animals, heads, small statuary and animals depicting the Chinese New Year. Clay medallions were made in the form of Greek, Roman and United States coins while others have signs of the Zodiac.

"Chop Marks" used as an imprinting stamp to identify some pottery made at the Merritt Island pottery. Each mark translates in Chinese to "Melvin Casper" or "Peggy Jamieson."

Pottery photographs from the files of the Merritt Island Pottery.

Chapter Twelve

Royal Hickman (1893-1969). Circa 1950. Photograph taken in
Tampa by Hickman's friend, Charles Adler.

Royal Hickman LTD
Tampa, Florida
1949-1956

In 1948 Royal Arden Hickman, a 56 year old ceramics designer of national reputation, and his wife Ruth, moved to Clearwater Beach planning on a quiet retirement in Florida. Hickman was an energetic man and his restless nature would shortly lead to the development of a Florida pottery that contributed some of this country's finest ceramic designs.

Royal Hickman was born on December 28, 1893 in Willamette, Oregon. As a young man Hickman was an accomplished outdoorsman, sailor and horseman, building a sailboat, rounding up wild horses with his father and winning silver spurs as a champion wrangler. In 1911 at the age of 18, "Hick" as he would later be called, moved to San Francisco to study at the Mark Hopkins Art Academy and then on to Hawaii. Hickman's love of nature played an important role in his later designs. With the beginning of World War I, Hickman returned home to enlist but was kept out of the Army by poor eyesight.

During the World War, Hick worked in a Navy shipyard in Tacoma, Washington as a draftsman. After the war he started a small construction company which took him to the Panama Canal and the Madden Dam. At the dam a gravel slide trapped Hickman briefly. As a result he developed heat stroke, which left him partially paralyzed. Hickman returned to California a sick man in need of rest and rehabilitation.

A cousin who had purchased the Garden City Pottery in San Jose, California, suggested that perhaps Hickman could help at the pottery. Hick, who had studied art, began working with the clay to strengthen his hands and to expand the pottery's production. He redesigned a chicken feeder and

A ceramic horse head unmarked but attributed to Royal Hickman, Ltd., Tampa, Florida. Height 13 1/4 inches, base 5 1/2 inches.

designed some dinnerware, thus beginning an association with pottery design and manufacture which would last the rest of his life.

In 1935 Hickman began the Ra Art (for Royal Arden) Pottery which he ran out of his garage. He developed a ceramics line for the G. & S. Gump Company department store of San Francisco and the J.H. Vernon Company of New York City. Ra Art quickly outgrew the garage and Hickman was convinced to move to New York.

In 1938 the Vernon Company sent Hickman to Europe to design crystal for the Kosta Glassbruck of Sweden. While in Europe he worked and traveled in Denmark, Italy and Czechoslovakia. (1)(2)

In Prague, Hickman produced Czechoslovakian pottery and art glass for export to the United States. When he got word that Hitler had moved into Austria and Czechoslovakia, Hickman tried to escape to Italy with a truckload of iron molds used in his glass work designs. He was caught and imprisoned in a Prague jail while the Germans checked him out. Hickman was a Methodist, but his name suggested he might be Jewish. After two weeks the Germans took his money and his molds and released him broke and with an ulcer. He made his way to Venice and the Isle of Murano where he was well known to the people at the Murano pottery. They provided money for his trip back to New York. (3)

That same year Hickman was hired as the Chief Designer for the prestigious Haeger Potteries of Dundee, Illinois. Haeger Pottery was one of the largest commercial potteries in the United States, with distribution in the best stores from New York to California. Royal Hickman developed the Royal Haeger line of pottery and in 1939 the Royal Haeger Lamp Company. That company developed an innovative and dramatic line of lamps, including Girl embracing Tarpon on Turtle, King Neptune Riding a Sailfish, Mermaid on Shell, Sunfish on Wave and Flying Fish lamps.

In 1939 Haeger was looking for a manufacturer's representative in New York City. Hickman traveled to a Fifth Avenue showroom where he met Ruth Rosenberg, described by a friend as "sweet and beautiful, a Hungarian but with gypsy blood."(4) They were married in 1941.

Hickman left the Haeger Pottery in 1944 and with partners, Frank Perry and Harvey Hamilton, started a lamp company, Royal Hickman Industries, in Chattanooga, Tennessee. The company was later sold to the Phil-Mar Lamp Company in Cleveland, Ohio and renamed Ceramic Arts Inc.

In 1949 Hickman began searching for the sun, sea and sand of his younger days. The Tampa Bay area was only a one day drive from Chattanooga. Hickman and his wife, Ruth, then moved to Clearwater Beach, Florida, bought a boat which they named the "Royal T" and planned to retire. In Tampa the Hickmans socialized with an old friend from Oregon, Melvin Lord and his wife, Carmen. (3)

Melvin Lord was the son of a prominent Oregon family and had served in World War II as a member of the OSS (Office of Special Services, the

A small ceramic fish with paper label, ROYAL HICKMAN Florida pottery of Florida Clay. Circa 1949-1953. Height 5 3/4 inches, base 3 1/2 inches.

Royal Hickman Horses head Lamp with matching finial. Circa 1949-1953.

Green glazed pouter pigeon vase, base embossed ROYAL HICKMAN 599. Height 8 inches, width 8 3/4 inches, base depth 7 inches. Circa 1949-1953.

A vase with fish on wave in gray glaze. Height 9 1/2 inches, base 4 inches by 6 inches. Embossed on base ROYAL HICKMAN FLORIDA 521. Circa 1949-1953.

forerunner of the CIA) in Spain, where he met Carmen. After closing a business in Pennsylvania, Lord moved his family to Tampa and Davis Island.

Hickman is described by his close family friend, Charles Adler, as "an attractive man, loud, raucous, a republican, a charismatic man that everybody liked, but who didn't like everybody, a restless man who was very commercial about his art." Hick met Adler through their mutual friend, Melvin Lord. One night Melvin Lord talking to Adler about Hickman, said, "That old son of a bitch if he doesn't like you, you'll know it right away." But Hickman and Adler were, as Charles says, *simpatico."* (4)

Being the restless, active man that he was, Hickman didn't stay retired long. He sold his boat, moved to Tampa to 12 Adalia, Davis Island and with his friend Melvin Lord, opened a pottery. Hickman was president and designer of the pottery, while Lord, who had a degree in engineering, was secretary, treasurer and in charge of production. The Tampa City Directory for 1950 lists Thero Bell as vice president.

The society section of the September 11, 1949 issue of the *Tampa Morning Tribune* carried the first notice of pottery production in Tampa. The ad announced that Royal Hickman Ltd. located at 11,115 Nebraska Avenue had ceramic figurines, vases, flower pots, lamps, dinnerware and aluminumware, all manufactured here in Tampa, on display and invited the public to inspect them. A week later on, September 18, the society section of the *Tampa Morning Tribune* carried a more formal announcement which read:

ROYAL HICKMAN LTD. ALREADY HAS WIDE RECOGNITION IN POTTERY ARTS. Has complete factory showroom.

Tampa's new ceramic plant, the only commercial pottery factory in Florida, is fast gaining recognition across the country for its fine designs and the quality of its products. A new factory showroom where the company's more than 150 new products are on display is open to

The Royal Hickman Pottery showroom, Nebraska Avenue, Tampa, Florida. Circa 1949-1953. Photo courtesy of Mrs. Carmen Lord, a friend of Hickman's in Tampa and the wife of Hickman's associate in the pottery, Melvin Lord.

everyone at 11,115 Nebraska Avenue, 1 1/2 miles north of the Tampa Dog Track on Highway 41.

Along with a display of new products, a complete line of exquisite table lamps designed and decorated personally by Royal Hickman is shown and offered for sale. Prices start at $3.90 for lamps complete with shade. It is impossible to buy lamps like these anyplace except directly from the factory.

Visitors are more than welcome. The company is happy to show the complete process and how a piece is turned, from a wet piece of clay into a beautiful piece of pottery. The factory is open week days through Friday until 4:30 p.m., and the showroom seven days a week until 6:00 p.m. Further information may be had by phoning 31-6075.

Come and see Mr. Hickman's new models that will shortly be finished pieces to be sold over the United States.

Royal Hickman pottery was, like the pottery he designed for Haeger, made from plaster of paris molds. Clay slip was poured into a plaster of paris copy mold and left standing until a thick shell had formed next to the copy mold. The copy mold then was turned upside down to drain off the liquid slip. The plaster of paris mold then absorbs moisture from the clay and as it dries, the copy pulls away from the original mold, is allowed to dry, finished, assembled if multiple pieces were involved, and then fired in a kiln. White bisqueware was then dipped or sprayed with a glaze and then fired again. Final hand painted decoration were then added and the pottery fired for a final time.

Life in Tampa was good for the Hickmans. According to Ruth Hickman, her husband loved Florida. He loved the outdoors, fishing and boating. The Hickmans traveled quite a bit. Once on a trip to New York City, they were walking down Fifth

Interior of the Royal Hickman Pottery showroom in Tampa with Mrs. Carmen Lord partly hidden by the shelves. Circa 1950. The showroom was located on Nebraska Avenue and the plant elsewhere.

Avenue past one of the famous department stores that handled ceramics like those designed by Royal, when Hickman said, "Oh, Ruth, look there! Give me a pencil, God damn it, I need to sketch this." "You old fool," Ruth replied, "That's your own design." (3)

Hickman loved to party with his friends and made frequent trips with them to Mexico and Cuba. His ulcer began to act up and while they drank martinis, he sipped on milkshakes. Finally Hick was admitted to Tampa General Hospital where he had surgery for his ulcer. During the operation the surgeons found a life threatening abdominal aortic aneurysm which was later repaired in Houston by the famous Dr. Michael DeBakey. Awakening from the anesthesia, Hickman hit his friend Adler in the stomach and said, "Well that's over, let's get back to work." (4)

While walking his pet Doberman with Adler, Hickman threw a stick across the street which the dog promptly returned. Hickman said, "If children behaved like dogs I'd consider having a few more."

The Korean War began in June of 1950 and sometime later Melvin Lord was called back to active duty in Washington, D.C. where he was placed in charge of the Spanish desk at the War Department. Lord's loss to the Hickman pottery would play an important role in later decisions.

On December 7, 1952 the *Tampa Tribune* carried a Hickman Ltd. ad for a "beautiful Madonna figurine made of Florida clay." A week later an ad suggested that Hickman ceramics were an excellent gift for Christmas and indicated the pottery would be open evenings until Christmas. On December 14, 1952 the *Tampa Tribune* warned of frost warnings for northern peninsular Florida with frost extending southward. Gainesville was expected to see 29°. Snow fell in Tallahassee and Pensacola.

The night of December 15 was a cold one in Tampa as well. Living in an apartment above the manufacturing plant was the plant manager, a Mr. Jeral Williams, his wife and two children, Linda and Butch. That night Mrs. Margaret Dunn, an aunt, was caring for the children, while the parents were out Christmas shopping. Most North Tampa homes were using extra electric power to keep their homes warm. A transformer immediately behind the pottery overheated, exploded and fell into the upper floor. The following day the *Tampa Morning Tribune* carried the following story.

POTTERY PLANT DESTROYED IN $100,000 FIRE

Three persons escaped unharmed last night from a fire which destroyed the pottery factory of Royal Hickman Ltd. Inc. and kept the entire Sulfur Springs Fire Department and one forestry service truck busy for more than three hours.

The loss was estimated at around $100,000 by Royal Hickman of 12 Adalia St., owner of the plant which employed 30 persons and manufactured art pottery objects for export to Canada and South and Central America, as well as for domestic sale.

Hickman said that it was impossible to determine how much of the loss was covered by insurance until a check of his business records is made.

Fire Chief George Pitts said the two-story sheet metal building which housed the production facilities of the company was destroyed as well as the pottery, molds and packaging equipment in the building.

The factory is located about a half mile behind the firm's retail salesrooms at 11,111 Nebraska Avenue.

The night of the fire is well remembered by Hickman's friend, Charles Adler. The Hickmans were completely devastated by the fire. They spent the night at Adler's home and got some warm clothing for plant superintendent Williams' children. (4)

Royal Hickman Calalilly Lamp with matching finial. Circa 1949-1953.

A bud like green glazed vase with paper label " ROYAL HICKMAN Florida Pottery of Florida Clay." Embossed on base ROYAL HICKMAN FLORIDA 547. Height 8 1/4 inches by 2 7/8 inches. Circa 1949-1953.

A vase in the form of a swan or duck in dark brown and light blue glazes. Height 13 1/2 inches, width 10 1/2 inches and depth 4 inches. Paper label in the form of an artists pallet reads, " ROYAL HICKMAN Florida Pottery of Florida Clay." Circa 1949-1953.

Royal Hickman Mare and Colt Lamp with matching finial. Circa 1949-1953.

Hickman had run ads in the Personal section advertising "summer bargains and factory rejects for sale." He had one cent sales and offered "This Ad worth $1 on any purchase of $10 or more on factory rejects." The ad from January 18 to 25 now announced,

> "LAST CHANCE! TO OWN A PIECE OF ROYAL HICKMAN POTTERY, FIRE DESTROYED OUR FACTORY ON DECEMBER 15TH AND NOW WE ARE HAVING FINAL SALE OF ALL STOCK ON HAND."

With the pottery gone, Hickman considered rebuilding, but with his partner, Melvin Lord, away in Washington, it would have been difficult for Hickman, who had come to Florida to retire, to rebuild alone. He had a world wide reputation as a designer and was called constantly for design help. He wanted to stay active in the ceramics industry. A General Armstrong from MacDill Air Force Base wanted to buy Hickman's home on Davis Island and the Vernon Pottery in California called. The Hickmans subsequently moved back to California where he worked as a design consultant for Vernon Potteries. Later he went to Guadalajara, Mexico, where he designed for Losa Fina, one of the world's largest manufacturers of dinnerware.

For his 76th birthday Ruth Hickman took over the Hilton Hotel in Guadalajara. Three waiters dressed as the famous Willard painting "Spirit of 76" and Hick, according to Mrs. Hickman, gave all the ladies present long and lingering kisses. Royal Hickman died in Guadalajara later that year, on September 1, 1969.(3)

When the art history of the World War II era in the United States is finally written, Royal Arden Hickman will be recognized as the "Tiffany" of his time. The ceramics produced in Tampa represent some of Hickman's best work and reflect the warmth and beauty of an early Florida that is slowly disappearing.

A bull in dark to light gray glaze. height 4 1/2 inches, width 2 inches, length 8 1/4 inches. Paper label, "ROYAL HICKMAN Florida Pottery of Florida Clay. Circa 1949-1953.

Lady on Turtle, Brown glazed flower holder with paper label, "ROYAL HICKMAN Florida Pottery of Florida Clay." Length 8 3/4 inches, width 3 1/2 inches, height 6 inches. Royal Hickman Pottery, Tampa, Florida. Circa 1949-1953.

A pelican ash tray in red glaze. 6 7/8 inches square. Paper label, "ROYAL HICKMAN Florida Pottery of Florida Clay." Circa 1949-1953.

Royal Hickman plate. Length 11 inches, width 7 1/2 inches. Embossed on base, ROYAL HICKMAN FLORIDA 582. Circa 1949-1953.

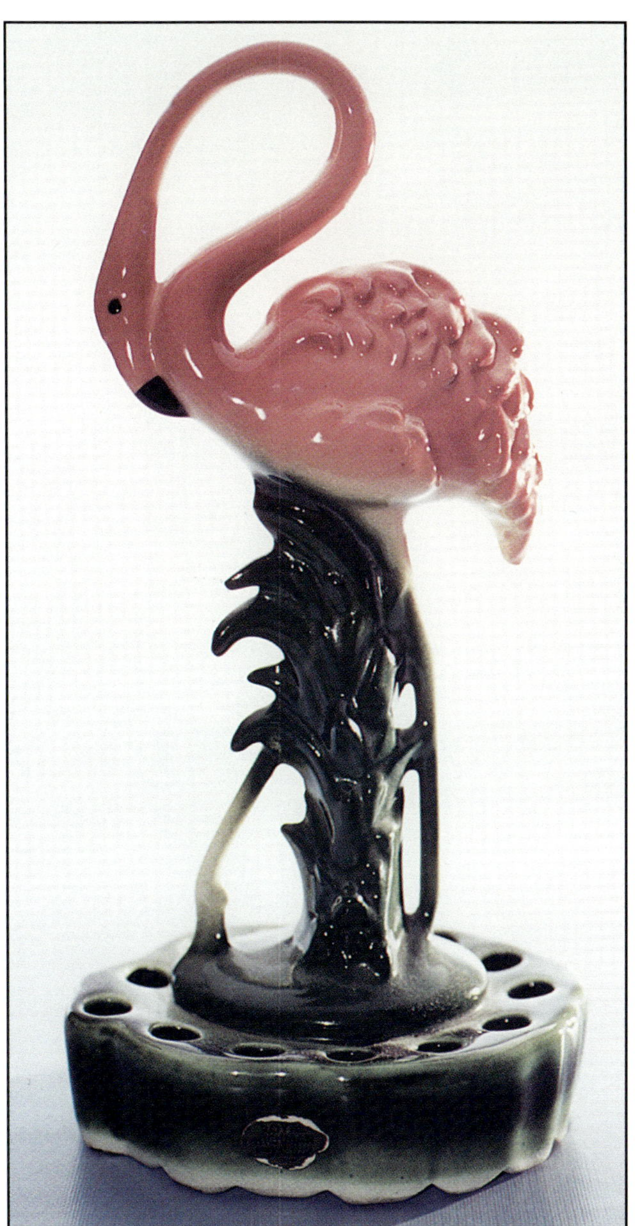

A flower holder in the form of a flamingo on a cabbage palm like base, height 10 inches, width 5 inches and depth 3 1/2 inches. Paper label in shape of an artist's pallet reads, "ROYAL HICKMAN FLORIDA POTTERY of Florida Clay." 13 holes in base for flowers.

Nassau centerpiece bowl with a wave crest on the form of a sea shell in purple glaze. Length 14 inches, width 7 inches, height 5 1/4 inches. Embossed on base ROYAL HICKMAN 614. Circa 1949-1953.

Seminole green glazed lodge planter 21 1/2 inches wide, 4 1/2 inches deep and 3 3/4 inches high. Unmarked. Attributed to Royal Hickman Ltd., Tampa, Florida. Circa 1949-1953. Frankel collection.

Royal Hickman Fighting Stallion Lamp in Petty Crystal Glaze with matching finial. Paper label reads, "Royal Hickman Petty Crystal Glaze." Circa 1949-1953. This lamp is pictured frequently in ads Hickman ran in the T*ampa Tribune.*

Royal Hickman Doe with Fawn Lamp in Petty Crystal Glaze. Circa 1949-1953.

Pelican wall pocket vase in yellow green glaze. Paper label, "ROYAL HICKMAN Florida Pottery of Florida Clay." Circa 1949-1953.

Fluted fan vase in green and white glaze, height 10 inches, width at top 10 inches and depth 4 inches. Embossed on base, "ROYAL HICKMAN, FLORIDA 602." Circa 1949-1953.

A yellow green glazed flower bowl with scalloped edges. Embossed on base, ROYAL HICKMAN FLORIDA 593.
Circa 1949-1953.

A green and white glazed gladiola vase. Embossed on base, "ROYAL HICKMAN FLORIDA 613. Height 10 3/8 inches, width
11 1/2 inches, depth 4 3/4 inches. Circa 1949-1953.

Embossed base of Royal Hickman Pottery. Note unglazed white bisque areas indicating Florida Clay. Identical pottery made in Chattanooga used a darker tan clay.

Royal Hickman paper label.

A vase with gray and light blue glaze 8 1/2 inches high, 5 1/2 inches wide and 3 1/4 inches deep. Embossed on base, "ROYAL HICKMAN, FLORIDA."

A light green glazed swan vase with leaf wings 10 1/2 inches high, 6 inches wide and 3 inches deep. Embossed on base, "ROYAL HICKMAN, FLORIDA 576."

IDENTIFICATION

A review of advertisements in the *Tampa Morning Tribune* by Royal Hickman Ltd. reveals the following ceramics were manufactured in Tampa.

<u>Lamp Bases</u>

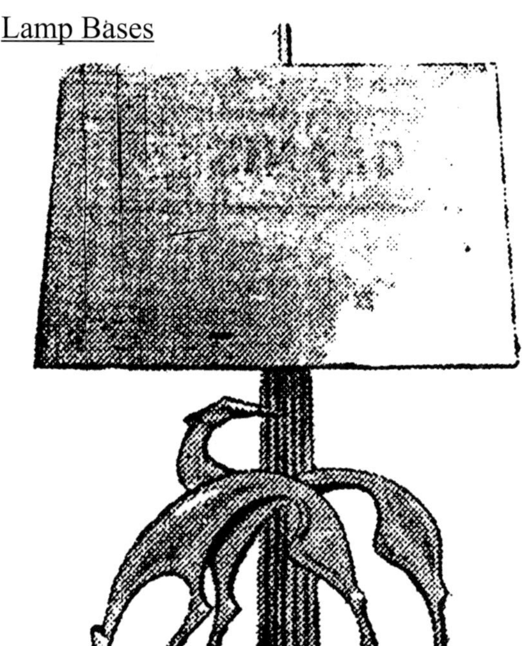

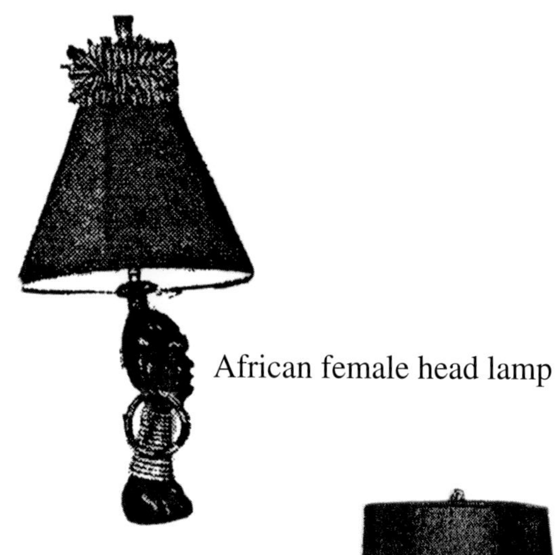

African female head lamp

Angel fish lamp (black and white striped fish) 29" high. $15.00

Zebra lamp

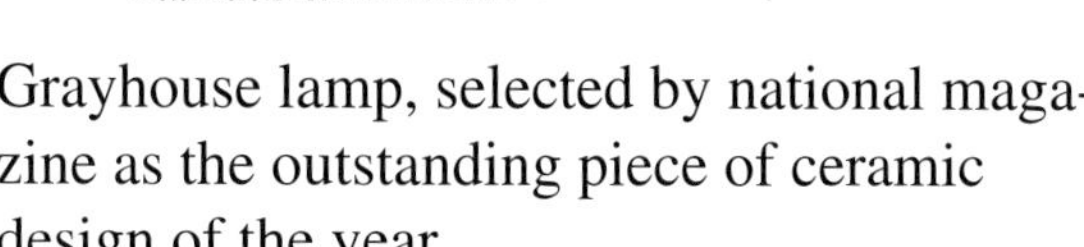

Grayhouse lamp, selected by national magazine as the outstanding piece of ceramic design of the year.

Black cat lamp, 29 1/2" high

Planter lamp base.

Joan of Arc lamp, 35" high, terra cotta head.

Horse's head (open mouth) lamp. 28" high, $25, terra cotta base (coca brown) horse's eyes and mane in turquoise,

Parrot fish lamp (black and white striped parrot fish) 25" high, $30.

Jaguar lamp (white jaguar with tree trunk and rock base in black) $35.

Figurines
1)	White cat with black spots $12.50
2)	Black cat
3)	White heron 18" high $25.00
4)	Madonna 11" high
5)	Flamingos

Planters and Vase
1)	Horse's head gladioli vase
2)	Pouter Pigeon vase 9" high
3)	Victorian shell vase 8 1/2" high 11 different colors
4)	Free form planter 4" high $3.00
5)	Fluted fan vase $7.50
6)	Key design vase 8 1/2" high $3.00
7)	Can Can Dancer vase 10" high, white skirt and base with dark blue dancing shorts and slippers $10.00
8)	Gladioli free form vase, available in green,

Free form modern table lamp.

leafgreen, highlighted gray and chestnut.   14"
$10.00
9)   Tropical leaf planter $5.00
10)   Glazed clay box planter (2 pieces square planters one fitting on top of the other, the bottom holding water)
11)   Swan planter 12 different colors 11" high
12)   Long Seminole Ledge planter (designed for mantles) 20" long tropical colors and drip glaze $6.50

<u>Bowls and Ashtrays</u>
1)   Various shaped ashtrays
2)   Nassau centerpiece bowl, hollow cast wave form on seashell
3)   Maize bowl, centerpiece, console or serving bowl designed from old rubbing stone used by Indians for grinding corn

Many different glazes were used including turquoise, coca brown, brown, chestnut, black, white, blue, gray, pink, green, leafgreen and yellow. Each piece was completely coated in glaze except for the bottom part resting on the kiln surface which retains its original bisque white appearance. Mixing of glazes gave a flowing dripping appearance to the final product. A "Petty crystal glaze" was used by Hickman on production in Tampa and Chattanooga. This glaze was designed by Hickman's business associate, chemist Frank Petty.

Many of these pieces survive without identifying paper labels. They can be distinguished by the type of clay used. In Florida, Hickman used a very white clay brought down from a kaolin mine near Gainesville so the unglazed bisque areas of Tampa pottery are white. Tennessee production used a darker clay and the bisque areas are tan in color.(5)

The final product was marked ROYAL HICKMAN, FLORIDA, or ROYAL HICKMAN or left unmarked. Many pieces are also marked with a catalogue or product identification number embossed into the base. A paper label was added in the shape of a small artist's pallet which reads, "ROYAL HICKMAN Florida Pottery of Florida Clay."

A pair of vases, pink and green glazes, each 5 1/4 inches high, 8 1/2 inches wide and 2 1/2 inches deep. Bases embossed, "ROYAL HICKMAN, FLORIDA." Circa 1949-1953.

Free form gladiola vase in green and yellow glaze. Height 14 1/4 inches, width 5 1/2 inches and depth 4 inches. Base embossed, "ROYAL HICKMAN, FLORIDA 574." Circa 1949- 1953.

A pair of Blue Herons, both with original paper labels that read, "ROYAL HICKMAN Florida Pottery of Florida Clay." Height 7 inches and 9 inches.

REFERENCE NOTES

CHAPTER 1

1. John L. McKinnon, *History of Walton County*, The
Bird Printing Co., Atlanta, Ga. 1911
Reprinted 1968, Kallman Publishing Co., Gainesville,
Florida page 129.
2. *Ibid* page 189
3. *Ibid* page 226
4. *Ibid* page 189
5. *Ibid* page 191
6. Ripley P. Bullen, *"Comments on Greer's Paper on
Alkaline Glazes."* The Conference on Historic Site
Archaeology Papers, Vol. 5. Part 1, 1970
7. Don Fredgant, *The Antique Journal*, June 1981.
T.B. Odom and J.W.Kohler: Two 19th Century West
Florida Potters.
8. *Ibid*
9. Conversation with Harold Gillis

CHAPTER 2

1. John H. Kohler, *Florida in the Gulf*, December
1925
2. *Bliss Quarterly,* Pensacola, January 1897
3. Pensacola *Commercial*, November 3, 1882
4. Pensacola *Journal*, March 16, 1916
5. Don Fredgant, *The Antiques Journal*. June, 1981. T.
B. Odom and J.W. Kohler: Two 19th Century West
Florida Potters.

CHAPTER 3

1. *Lake Butler 1893-1993*, Stepping Back In Time,
Project of Lake Butler Rotary Club 1993
Touring Through Town 1893-1993 Celebrating the
Incorporation of Lake Butler, Florida
2. *Minutes of Old Providence Baptist Church*, Providence, Union County, Florida Established 1833
3. Don Fredgant, *The Antique Journal*, The York
Pottery, Lake Butler, Florida, November 1980
4. *Confederate Military History*, Chapter 8
5. Conversation with Mrs. Hal York Maines, 1997
6. The Union County *Times*, April 8, 1938
7. Ripley P. Bullen, "Comments on Greer's Paper on
Alkaline Glazes." The Conference on Historic Site
Archaeology Papers, Vol. 5. Part 1, 1970
8. Bradford *County Telegraph*, June 29, 1888
9. *Ibid* May 17, May 31, June 7, June 14, 1889

10. *Ibid* July 26, 1889
11. Ripley P. Bullen, "Comments on Greer's Paper
on Alkaline Glazes."
12. Bradford *County Telegraph*, July 11, 1890
13. Terry Taylor and Terry and Kay Lawrence,
*Collectors Encyclopedia of SALT GLAZE STONE-
WARE*, Collector Books, 1997.
14. Joan Leibowitz, *Yellow Ware: The Transitional
Ceramic*, Schiffer Publishing Ltd., Atglen, PA. 1985

CHAPTER 4

1. Ollie Z. Fogarty, *They Called It Fogartyville,*
Theo. Gaus' Sons, Inc. Brooklyn, N.Y. 1972
2. Manatee River *Evening Journal*, August 27, 1915
3. *Ibid* November 19, 1915
4. Mrs. Lawrence Dowd, in a speech given to a local
civic club in Bradenton, January 15, 1969
5. Manatee River *Journal*, May 11, 1916
6. *Ibid* October 5, 1916
7. *Ibid* Janurary 4, 1917
8. *Ibid* December 27, 1917
9. St.Petersburg *Times*, February 3,1918
10. Tampa *Morning Tribune*, January 30,1921
11. Manatee River *Journal*, April 28, 1921

CHAPTER 5

1. Conversations with Madeline Graack Peterson,
1996
2. Manatee River *Journal*, August 4, 1921
3. Manatee River and Bradentown *Herald*, February
, 1922
4. Manatee River *Journal* June 29, 1922
5. *Ibid* January 1, 1923
6. *Ibid* March 15, 1923
7. *Ibid* November 8, 1923
8. Manatee River *Journal*, July 27, 1914
9. Manatee River *Journal* Sept 21, 1914
10. Conversations with Madeline Graack Peterson,
1996

CHAPTER 6

1. Orlando *Morning Sentinel* July 2, 1921
2. *Ibid* September 30,1921
3. *Ibid* December 23, 1922
4. *Ibid* March 12, 1922
5. *Ibid* August 9, 1922

7. *Ibid* December 17, 1922
8. *Ibid* December 23, 1922
9. Eve Bacon, *Orlando A Centennial History*, The Mickler Publishing House, Chuluota, Florida 1975
10. Orlando Morning *Sentinel* March 21, 1923
11. *Ibid* May 11,1923
12. *Ibid* November 28, 1923
13. *Ibid* December 16 through 21, 1923
14. *Ibid* September 4, 1924
15. *Ibid* October 5. 1924
16. *Ibid* February 17,1925
17. *Ibid* March 17, 1925
18. *Ibid* February 13,1927
19. Joe Y. Cheney, In a hand written letter in the files of the Orange County Historical Society. May 1974
20. *The Old Pottery*, Orange County Historical Quarterly, June 1975.
21. Orlando Morning *Sentinel* August 30, 1931

CHAPTER 7

1. Alva Johnston, *The Legendary Mizners*. Farrar, Straus & Young. New York, 1953.
2. Alex Waugh, The Mizner Industries. Personal memoir of Mr. Waugh in the files of the Historical Society of Palm Beach.
3. Alice DeLarma in a hand written note in the files of the Historical Society of Palm Beach.
4. Palm Beach *Weekly News*, December 13, 1918.
5. Prospectus of Mizner Industries in the files of the Historical Society of Palm Beach.

CHAPTER 8

1. St. Petersburg Ciy Directory 1916
2. Converstions with Alvin Kohler, son of Joseph Kohler.
3. Letter in the possession of Alvin Kohler.

CHAPTER 9

1.Conversations with Mrs. Dean Crary at Bluff Springs in 1998.
2. John Williamson Crary, Sr. Reminiscences of The Old South. 1834-1866.
3. Don Fredgant, *The Antiques Journal*. April 1980. Florida's Crary Pottery 1933-1939.

CHAPTER 10

1. Conversation with Madeline Graack Peterson at Fernandina Beach, 1997.
2. Telephone conversation with William B. Rae.
3. Telephone conversation with Al Scudder.

CHAPTER 11

1. The Cocoa *Tribune,* Friday April 1, 1966.
2. Miami *Herald*, Brevard County edition, January 6, 1940.
3. Conversations with Wilbur Casper.
4. Orlando *Evening Star*, Monday, December 13, 1948.
5. Melbourne *Times*, Friday, March 4, 1949.
6. Cocoa *Tribune*, Friday,. November 11, 1955.
7. Miami *Herald*, Sunday, April 8, 1956.
8. A letter in the Merritt Island Pottery file from Mrs. Pancoast, Chairman Fourth Miami National Ceramic Exhibition, to Esther Jamieson, on University of Miami stationery.
9. *Today's Sunrise,* Sunday, November 23,1969.
10. Miami Herald, Brevard County edition, Sunday, August 6, 1961
11. ibid, August 6, 1961
12. ibid, Business Guide, March 13, 1962.

CHAPTER 12

1. Lee Garmon, Doris Frizzell, *Collecting Royal Haeger*. Collector Books, Paducah, Kentucky 1989
2. David D. Dilley, *Haeger Potteries Through The Years*. L.W. Book Sales, Gas City, Indiana, 1997.
3. Telephone conversation with Ruth Hickman, 1998.
4. Conversations with Charles Adler, Davis Island, Tampa, Florida 1998.
5.Conversations with Keith Kuperman an antique dealer who specializes in Haeger, Hickman pottery.